Für Theodor und Simone
Ch. St.

Als Archäologin in Syrien

As an Archaeologist in Syria

Christine Strube

Als Archäologin in Syrien

Erfahrungen und Ereignisse

1971–1980 und 1997–2007

As an Archaeologist in Syria

Experiences and Events

1971–1980 and 1997–2007

Bibliografische Information der Deutschen Nationalbibliothek
Die Deutsche Nationalbibliothek verzeichnet diese Publikation in der Deutschen Nationalbibliografie; detaillierte bibliografische Daten sind im Internet über http://dnb.dnb.de abrufbar.

 Dieses Werk ist unter der Creative Commons-Lizenz 4.0 (CC BY-SA 4.0) veröffentlicht. Die Umschlaggestaltung unterliegt der Creative Commons-Lizenz CC BY-ND 4.0.

Diese Publikation ist auf https://www.propylaeum.de dauerhaft frei verfügbar (Open Access).
urn: urn:nbn:de:bsz:16-propylaeum-ebook-1024-7
doi: https://doi.org/10.11588/propylaeum.1024

Publiziert bei
Universität Heidelberg/Universitätsbibliothek
Proylaeum – Fachinformationsdienst Altertumswissenschaften
Grabengasse 1, 69117 Heidelberg
https://www.uni-heidelberg.de/de/impressum

Text © 2022, Christine Strube

Umschlagillustrationen: Vorderseite Kalksteinfelsen nahe Banaqfur im Nordsyrischen Kalksteinmassiv, Rückseite Haus des 6. Jahrhunderts im Djebel Zawiye, der südliche Region des Nordsyrischen Kalksteinmassivs.

ISBN 978-3-96929-158-0 (Hardcover)
ISBN 978-3-96929-142-9 (PDF)

Vorwort

Mit Berichten und Fotos zur Situation in Qalʿat Simʿan und zahlreichen Ruinenorten des Nordsyrischen Kalksteinmassivs informierte 2016–2020 die ‚Syrians for Heritage Association' über Bombardierungen durch Kampfflugzeuge, Granat- und Raketeneinschläge, Raubgrabungen, Steinraub, Antikenraub. Die positiven Erinnerungen an die langjährige Tätigkeit in Syrien wurden überlagert von dem Schock über die tiefgehenden Veränderungen in den mir vertrauten Orten.

Die Publikation meines letzten Projektes begleiteten die Berichte über die Ereignisse in Syrien. Sie war 2015 fertiggestellt und ich konnte sie mit dem Grabungsteam bei einem Essen in meinem italienischen Stammrestaurant feiern. Danach begann ich negative wie positive Erinnerungen aufzuschreiben – für meinen Sohn Julian und als eine Art Medizin auch für mich. Ich versuchte zu begreifen: Wie waren deine Erfahrungen in den Jahrzehnten vor 2011? Welche Erinnerungen hast du an Gespräche und Situationen während der letzten Grabungskampagnen in al-Andarin?

Auf die vielen Fotos und Zeichnungen meiner Publikationen habe ich in den folgenden Berichten nicht zurückgegriffen. Obwohl sie in einem Institut meines Faches archiviert sind, hätte ich eine große Auswahl treffen können. Doch ich hoffe, dass die Berichte auch mit den wenigen, stichwortartig eingefügten Fotos anschaulich sind. Ich zitiere hier die arabischen Ortsnamen nicht in der in französischen Publikationen vorherrschenden Umschrift, die ich auch in meinen Publikationen übernommen habe. Im Blick auf die Zweisprachigkeit meiner Berichte habe ich – *nolens volens* – die Zitierweise ge-wählt, die in englischen Publikationen bevorzugt wird. Ich danke Aurelia Badde für die englische Übersetzung des Textes.

Zu viele Mitarbeiter und Unterstützer, die in den Abbildungen erscheinen, leben nicht mehr. Sie gehören zu den hier erzählten Ereignissen und Erinnerungen und darum folgen auf die Abbildungen von Orten und Monumenten einige Tafeln mit Personen – *in memoriam*.

Ich danke meinem Sohn Julian, Renate Marzolff und Achim Arbeiter, die mich überzeugt haben, dass es sinnvoll sein könnte, diese Berichte zu publizieren. Ich habe erst nach den Ereignissen in Qalʿat Simʿan begriffen, dass sie ein kleiner Beitrag für die in die Zukunft weisenden Projekte der ‚SIMAT', ‚Syrians for Heritage Association', und des ‚Syrian Heritage Archive Projekt' sein könnten.

Ich bin Katrin Bemmann und ihren Mitarbeitern dankbar für die Annahme und Unterstützung meiner Publikation. Die notwendigen Schritte für eine Veröffentlichung als e-Book haben mich überfordert, doch sie wurden bewältigt von Fedor Schlimbach – ihm gilt mein besonderer Dank.

Heidelberg 14. Februar 2022.

Inhalt

Vorwort 5

Inhalt 7

Einleitung 9

Das erste Projekt: Aufnahmen im Nordsyrischen Kalksteinmassiv 13

    1971. Aufbruch nach Syrien 13

        Gründung des Institut Français und die Jahre nach der Unabhängigkeit Syriens 14

    1973. Neuorganisation der *Mission archéologique de Haute Syrie*; „*retraite*" von Tchalenko 17

    1974. Erste Kampagne im Kalksteinmassiv 18

    1975. Beginn des Bürgerkriegs; zweite Kampagne im Kalksteinmassiv 25

        Fahrt nach Izmir 29

    1976. Aufenthalt in Rom. Auswertung der Arbeitskampagnen 30

    1977. Dritte Kampagne im Kalksteinmassiv 31

        Nach einem Unfall, Transport in das Gefängnis von Hama 32

    1977. Rückfahrt mit dem Schiff von Beirut aus über Alexandria nach Venedig 34

    1978. Ende der Aufnahmen in Qalʿat Simʿan 35

    1979. Vierte Kampagne: Aufnahmen in der Madrasa al-Hallawiya und in Qasr ibn Wardan 36

    1980. Nacharbeit im Kalksteinmassiv; Vorbereitung einer Syrien-Ausstellung 38

    1989–1990. Reise zu den Ruinenorten des Bergmassivs, die jetzt zur Türkei gehören 39

    2016–2019. Zur Situation in Qalʿat Simʿan nach 2011 41

    2019. Publikation der Restaurierungen von G. Tchalenko in Qalʿat Simʿan durch J. Tchalenko 42

Das zweite Projekt: Grabungsarbeiten in al-Andarin, dem antiken Androna 45

    1996. Rückkehr nach Syrien; Vorbereitung der Ausgrabung 45

    1997. Reise nach Syrien im Frühjahr. Im Sommer Survey und geodätische Vermessung 48

        Der Nachbarort Sammakiya und die Familie Sammakiya 50

        Anwerbung lokaler Arbeiter und Neueinstellung von Antikenwächtern 51

    1998. Erste Grabungskampagne; Bohrung nach Grundwasser 53

        Bau des Grabungshauses 54

Als Archäologin in Syrien

    1998. Erste Aktivitäten der drei Grabungsteams 56

    2000. Erweiterung der Aktivitäten der drei Grabungsteams 56

        Mitarbeiter des deutschen Grabungsteams; Kontakte zwischen den drei Grabungsteams ... 58

    1997–2007. Probleme des Ruinenortes: Beduinenzelte, tausende von Schafen und Autopisten 59

    2001. Autounfall vor Grabungsbeginn; Anschlag am 11. September 2001 in New York 59

    2002. Rückkehr von A. Sammakiya; Kultivierung der Ländereien im Umland von Androna 60

    2003. Fortsetzung der Grabung 63

    2004. Restaurierungsarbeiten in Androna 65

    2005. Situation der Hausgrabung nach der Freilegung eines Bodenmosaiks 66

    2006. Ausgrabung der Kastronkirche; Feier des ‚Tages der Wüste / Steppe' im Frühjahr 66

        Situation der Kirche im Hof des Kastrons 67

    2007. Kampagne der Fundbearbeitung 68

    2010. Erste Kampagne in der Hauptkirche von Androna 69

    2016. Zerstörungen durch den IS im Kastron von Androna 69

    Überlegungen zur ‚*Syrians for Heritage Association*' und dem ‚*Syrian Heritage Archive Projekt*' ... 71

Anmerkungen 75
Literaturverzeichnis 81

As an Archaeologist in Syria 85

Tafeln / Plates

Einleitung

> *„Es gibt eine Göttin der Erinnerung, Mnemosyne, aber keine des Vergessens. Doch es sollte sie geben, denn sie sind Zwillingsschwestern, Zwillingskräfte. Sie nehmen uns in die Mitte, und bis zu unserem Tod kämpfen sie um die Herrschaft über uns und streiten sich darüber, wer wir sind"* (Richard Holmes: A Meander through Memory and Forgetting).

Fast zwei Jahrzehnte habe ich in Nordsyrien und in einer Region Zentralsyriens gearbeitet. Die Ergebnisse stellen den Hauptteil meiner Lebensarbeit als Archäologin dar.

In den Jahren 1997–2007 fanden mit verschiedenen Grabungsteams aufwendige Grabungsarbeiten in al-Andarin statt. Meine letzte Publikation zu archäologischer Arbeit in Syrien berichtete 2018 von den Zerstörungen in al-Andarin durch den Islamischen Staat[1].

Im Jahr 2016 erreichte mich der erste Bericht über Zerstörungen in Qalʿat Simʿan, die Teile des 1936–1942 durch Georges Tchalenko restaurierten Pilgerzentrums betrafen (Taf. 12b. 13. 15), sowie Informationen über die katastrophale Situation in zahlreichen Ruinenorten des Nordsyrischen Kalksteinmassivs[2].

Schon vor 2014 hatten die Kämpfe in der Altstadt von Aleppo durch Granateinschläge und Brand den Innenraum der einzigen wenigstens teilweise erhaltenen frühbyzantinischen Kirche des antiken Beroea, der Madrasa al-Hallawiya, zerstört[3]. Ich hatte 1979 seine Kapitelle gemeinsam mit der Architektin Heike Fastje mit Fotos und Zeichnungen aufgenommen (Taf. 9).

Wie geht man mit solchen Erfahrungen um?

1905 hatte Gertrude Bell eine Reise über Homs und Hama nach Aleppo gemacht und war auf diesem Weg durch zahlreiche Siedlungen des Nordsyrischen Kalksteinmassivs gekommen, die viele Jahre später zu meinem Forschungsgebiet wurden.

Ich schlage in ihrem Bericht das Kapitel über Hama auf, geradezu süchtig nach einem Blick in die Zeit vor den tiefgreifenden Zerstörungen der letzten Jahre, und sehe als erstes ein Foto der Altstadt von Hama[4]. Ich hatte dieselbe Ansicht 1980 aufgenommen (Taf. 1a) vor der Zerstörung der Altstadt durch die syrische Luftwaffe im Jahr 1982. Zehn Jahre später fuhr ich auf der neu errichteten Asphaltstraße an den Ruinen einzelner Häuser der Altstadt vorbei, hinauf zum luxuriösen Sham-Hotel.

Als ich ein Jahr später zu Nacharbeiten in das Nordsyrische Kalksteinmassiv kam, hatte sich dort die Situation verändert: Im Rahmen des Tourismus-Programms der syrischen Regierung waren zahlreiche kleine Asphaltstraßen angelegt worden. Sie führten nun zu den antiken Ruinenorten und hatten die Ausplünderung der Kirchen und Häuser durch den Abtransport von Kapitellen und Türstürzen mit Pickups leicht gemacht.

Die Zerstörung Syriens in den Kämpfen nach 2011 verdrängte meine negativen Erfahrungen aus den Jahrzehnten des vergangenen Jahrtausends. Doch mit den Nachrichten und Fotos, die mich nach und nach erreichten, wurden sie ein Teil der Fragen nach dem Sinn meiner archäologischen Arbeiten und das heißt auch, nach der Bedeutung von älteren Fotos, Zeichnungen und Dokumentationen für zukünftige Restaurierungen und Forschungen in Syrien.

Ich beschreibe im Folgenden die Gesamtsituation, die ich 1971–1980 im Nordsyrischen Kalksteinmassiv und 1997–2007 in der innersyrischen Wüstensteppe nordöstlich von Hama angetroffen habe. Sollten dort in einigen Jahren archäologische Arbeiten wieder möglich werden, so wird sich in beiden Regionen die Situation grundlegend von der unterscheiden, die ich damals erlebt habe.

In meinen wissenschaftlichen Publikationen habe ich nur selten über die Arbeit hinausgehende Ereignisse und Erfahrungen angesprochen. Es könnte sinnvoll sein, sie nun durch einen Bericht über die Gesamtsituation zu ergänzen, die ich im Nordsyrischen Kalksteinmassiv und in der innersyrischen Wüstensteppe nordöstlich von Hama angetroffen habe.

Erst nach den beiden Berichten werde ich mit den wichtigsten Ergebnissen vorausblicken auf eventuelle zukünftige Arbeiten, und das heißt, auf die nach der Zerstörung der Infrastruktur in allen Bereichen Syriens vollkommen offene Situation. Die Überlegungen zur Funktion vor vielen Jahren angefertigter Fotos, Zeichnungen und Dokumentationen wird zu der ‚Syrians for Heritage Association' und dem ‚Syrian Heritage Archive Projekt' führen.

In meinem Bericht über die Jahre 1971–1980 blicke ich im Folgenden zurück auf die Reise durch Nordsyrien von Gertrude Bell, die Aufnahmen der ‚Princeton University Archaeological Expeditions to Syria' kurz vor und kurz nach 1900[5], die Neuerungen in der französischen Mandatszeit und die Veränderungen in den Jahrzehnten nach 1946 und vor 1971. Meine Erfahrungen führen nicht zu Grabungen der Vorderasiatischen Archäologie oder Zentren der römischen

Zeit (z. B. Kanawat, Palmyra), sondern zur spätantik-frühbyzantinischen und frühislamischen Zeit.

Der Bericht über die Jahre 1997–2007 wird in eine ganz andere Situation führen: zu den Grabungsarbeiten in al-Andarin der zentralsyrischen Wüstensteppe. Al-Andarin, das antike Androna, war der Ort, zu dem ich am Ende meiner Arbeiten im nordsyrischen Kalksteinmassiv kam[6]. Ich hatte 1980 eventuelle Grabungsarbeiten in al-Andarin in der Generaldirektion in Damaskus diskutiert und dort schließlich 1996 eine internationale Zusammenarbeit organisiert.

Das erste Projekt: Aufnahmen im Nordsyrischen Kalksteinmassiv

1971. Aufbruch nach Syrien

Nach langjährigem Studium der Klassischen Archäologie und Alten Geschichte hatte ich, angeregt durch einen Aufenthalt in Istanbul im Jahr 1965, ein Zweitstudium aufgenommen. Es waren diese Wochen in der ehemaligen byzantinischen Hauptstadt, die mich so tief beeindruckt hatten, dass ich nach meiner Rückkehr ein Studium der Byzantinischen Geschichte und Archäologie in München begann: Nicht Zentraleuropa als ‚Nabel der Welt', sondern das Gegenüber von Europa und dem Vorderen Orient waren für mich entscheidend geworden.

Mein erstes Projekt nach der Promotion benannte sich „*Einsatz von Photogrammetrie und Datenverarbeitung bei der Aufnahme umfangreicher Architekturbestände*" und wurde für ein Jahr von der Stiftung zur Förderung der Wissenschaften in Bayern finanziert. In seinem Zentrum stand das Nordsyrische Kalksteinmassiv mit seinen ungewöhnlich gut erhaltenen Bauten des 1.–7. Jahrhunderts n. Chr.

Die ersten Aufnahmen von Bauten im Kalksteinmassiv waren Teil der Publikationen zahlreicher Bauten Nord- und Südsyriens nach den Expeditionen der Princeton University unter der Leitung von Howard Crosby Butler[7]. Die nächste große Etappe in der Erforschung des Kalksteinmassivs war die dreibändige Publikation von Georges Tchalenko: „*Villages antiques de la Syrie du Nord*" – eine beispielhafte Erforschung aller Aspekte dieser reichen Kulturlandschaft[8].

1971 nahm ich Kontakt zu Georges Tchalenko, dem Leiter der Mission Archéologique de Haute Syrie auf, stellte mein Projekt vor und wurde zusammen mit dem Studenten der Architektur Alexander Wetzig eingeladen, an einer Nacharbeitungskampagne in 46 Siedlungen des Kalksteinmassivs teilzunehmen. Geplant war die Verbesserung und Erweiterung der Fotodokumentation für Tchalenkos zweite große Publikation: „*Églises syriennes à bêma*". Mit den großartigen Erfahrungen dieser Reise in alle Regionen des Bergmassivs hatte sich viel für mich verändert. Der Bestand der erhaltenen Kirchen, Häuser und Grabbauten war überwältigend (Taf. 5. 7a. b) und viel umfangreicher, als die Publikationen erwarten ließen. Ich erkannte, dass dem Einsatz einer wie immer gearteten Datenverarbeitung die beispielhafte Gesamtaufnahme mindestens einer Siedlung vorangehen sollte. Daher reichte ich bei der Stiftung die Ergebnisse für ein Beschreibungssystem in Deutsch, Englisch und Französisch ein und begann mit Georges Tchalenko die Planung der Gesamtaufnahme einer Siedlung unter seiner Leitung und angeschlossen an das Institut Français. Er hatte bereits für drei Siedlungen einen topographischen Gesamtplan mit Grundrissen der einzelnen Bauten erarbeitet. Für einen der Orte sollten alle an der Oberfläche greifbaren Bauten unter Einsatz der Photogrammetrie aufgenommen, durch Teilgrabungen ergänzt und mit analytischen Beschreibungen in einer Gesamtdarstellung erfasst werden.

Als sich jedoch 1972 abzeichnete, dass die geplante Gesamtaufnahme einer Siedlung als französisch-deutsche Zusammenarbeit und unter der Leitung von Georges Tchalenko nicht würde stattfinden können, arbeitete ich auf der Basis der 1971 gemachten Erfahrungen ein Projekt zur Erforschung der Kapitelle in den Kirchen des 4.–6. Jahrhunderts im Nordsyrischen Kalksteinmassiv aus.

In den 70er Jahren des letzten Jahrhunderts gab es in Syrien keine Abteilung des Deutschen Archäologischen Instituts. Im Mittelpunkt der laufenden wie der geplanten archäologischen Aktivitäten in Syrien und im Libanon stand das Institut Français in Beirut. Hier ist es nötig, dass ich die Situation schildere, die ich 1971 antraf, und kurz auf die politischen Ereignisse vor und nach der Gründung des Instituts eingehe.

Gründung des Institut Français und die Jahre nach der Unabhängigkeit Syriens

Die Forderungen nach der Unabhängigkeit Syriens in den Jahren nach Ende des ersten Weltkrieges fanden nach der Niederlage der syrischen Armee gegen die französischen Mandatstruppen bei Maysalun, der Exilierung von König Faysal und der gewaltsamen Niederschlagung der folgenden Aufstände ein vorläufiges Ende. Der Völkerbund erkannte 1922 das französische Mandat über Syrien und Libanon an. 1929 war Henri Seyrig zum Directeur Général des Antiquités de Syrie et du Liban ernannt worden. Er unterbrach seine Arbeit im Orient während des Zweiten Weltkrieges mit Aufgaben in Mexiko und Amerika und kehrte 1945 für die Gründung des Institut Français d´Archéologie de Beyrouth zurück. Im April 1946 erklärte der syrische Präsident die Unabhängigkeit Syriens. Das Institut Français war nun rechtlich der Antikenkommission in Damaskus unterstellt, doch wurden weiterhin alle Entscheidungen über archäologische Arbeiten in Syrien mit dem Institut Français abgesprochen. Es war Henri Seyrig, zuerst Direktor des Service des Antiquités en Syrie et au Liban und danach Direktor des Institut Français in Beirut (1945–1967), der mit seiner umfassenden Toleranz und Weitsicht archäologische Missionen verschiedener Nationen über viele

Das erste Projekt: Aufnahmen im Nordsyrischen Kalksteinmassiv

Jahre hin gefördert hat: die Mission der Belgier in Apamea, der Briten in Bosra, der Dänen in Hama, der Deutschen in Tell Halaf. 1934 übertrug er Georges Tchalenko, einem emigrierten russischen Architekten, Restaurierungsarbeiten in Qalʿat Simʿan, Qalbloze und zahlreichen anderen Orten Syriens.

Eine ausführliche Biographie und einen Bericht über die Jahre der Zusammenarbeit seines Vaters mit Henri Seyrig publizierte 2019 der Sohn von Georges Tchalenko[10]. Ich nenne nur einige Daten der Biographie, die der Ankunft in Syrien vorangingen: Georges Tchalenko war nach seiner Emigration 1922 zum Studium der Architektur an die Technische Hochschule in Braunschweig gegangen, arbeitete nach Abschluss des Studiums bei einigen Projekten mit Alexander Klein, Walter Gropius und Mies van der Rohe zusammen und wurde 1931 gegen alle Widerstände Leiter des Konstruktionsbüros der Technischen Hochschule in Braunschweig. 1933 verließ er Deutschland. In Jerusalem nahm er das Angebot von Harald Ingholt an, als Architekt bei der dänischen Ausgrabung in Hama mitzuarbeiten. Im Rahmen dieses Projekts traf er 1934 mit Henri Seyrig zusammen (Taf. 37a).

Ich kehre zurück zu der Planung der Aufnahmen im Kalksteinmassiv. In ihren Publikationen hatten nicht nur Howard Crosby Butler, sondern auch Jean Lassus und Georges Tchalenko über den intensiven Raub vor allem der Kapitelle in Nord- und Zentralsyrien berichtet[11]. Kapitelle konnten aus nicht zu weit abgelegenen Ruinenorten leicht abtransportiert werden, da sie ohne Grabungsarbeiten erreichbar waren (Taf. 7b). Sie waren ihrer Qualität wegen nicht nur bei Privatsammlern beliebt und konnten nicht nur in Europa, sondern auch in Amerika in Empfangshallen von Hotels oder in Gartenanlagen als Tischstützen bewundert werden. Nach den Eindrücken der Reise von 1971 mit hunderten von Kapitellen im Versturz der Kirchen erschien mir die Erforschung dieser so wichtigen Befunde der Baudekoration dringend erforderlich.

Den Aufnahmen im Bergmassiv sollte die Aufnahme der Kapitelle in der Sammlung von Henri Pharaon in Beirut vorangehen. Ich hatte sie 1971 kennengelernt (Taf. 4). Die 210 Kapitelle der Sammlung stammten überwiegend aus dem Kalksteinmassiv. In einem Brief an Henri Pharaon bat ich 1973 um eine Aufnahmegenehmigung für die Kapitelle seiner Sammlung. Nach seiner Zusage fragte ich beim Institut Français an, ob Ernest Will einen Antrag auf *„Untersuchungen zu den Kapitellen in den Kirchen des 4.–6. Jahrhunderts im Nordsyrischen Kalksteinmassiv"* bei der Generaldirektion Syrischer Altertümer in Damaskus unterstützen würde.

Als Archäologin in Syrien

Nach positiver Antwort von beiden Seiten stellte ich den Antrag für *„Studien zu den Kapitellen in den Kirchen des 4–6. Jhs. im nordsyrischen Kalksteinmassiv"* bei der Generaldirektion Syrischer Altertümer, der überraschend schnell bewilligt wurde. Mein folgender Antrag auf ein Habilitationsstipendium bei der Deutschen Forschungsgemeinschaft wurde im Frühjahr 1974 bewilligt. Schon im April 1974 beförderte ich gemeinsam mit dem Fotografen Helmut Loose den VW-Bus mit der Turkish Maritime Lines nach Beirut, begann die Arbeit in Beirut und bereitete die erste Kampagne im Kalksteinmassiv vor.

Im Frühjahr 1974 wurden alle Kapitelle der Sammlung Pharaon vermessen und von Helmut Loose mit 6×6-Kameras aufgenommen. Der Photograph und ich wohnten in sehr guter Atmosphäre im Deutschen Orientinstitut und wurden von Henri Pharaon verwöhnt: Jeden Tag bekocht von mehreren Köchen – klassisch Arabisch, klassisch Europäisch, Russisch – unter der Aufsicht seines *major domus*. Mit Helga Seeden von der American University Beirut fuhren wir nach Tyros, Byblos und in die Drusendörfer des Libanon, mit Georges Tchalenko nach Damaskus und Resafa.

Kurz vor Abschluss meiner Kapitellaufnahmen bat mich Henri Pharaon, ihn zu einem der Depots des größten Antikenhändlers in Beirut zu begleiten: Ein Dutzend Basaltkapitelle seien eingetroffen, ein Kapitelltypus, der in seiner Sammlung fehle. Vor ihrem Transport nach Europa oder Amerika wollte er einige für seine Sammlung auswählen. In dem großen Lager erlebte ich einen großen Schock: sehr viele Kapitelle, ganze Türstürze, große Fußbodenmosaike in kleine Quadrate zerschnitten – sie waren alle aus Syrien geraubt. Nach einem Satz zu Pharaon *„alle Basaltkapitelle sind gut"* drehte ich mich um und verließ die Halle. Ich ahnte damals nicht, dass dieser Schock nur die Einleitung zu einer langen Kette von Erfahrungen mit Antikenraub in Syrien war.

Für meine Aufnahmen im Kalksteinmassiv waren diese Erfahrungen mit der großen Anzahl der Kapitelle in der Sammlung und die Konfrontation mit dem maßlosen Antikenraub in der Lagerhalle im Hafen von Beirut entscheidend: Einige Basaltkapitelle mussten von Henri Pharaon schnell gekauft werden, bevor sie auf Schiffe Richtung Europa verfrachtet werden konnten.

Die Arbeit in der Sammlung Pharaon war die beste Vorbereitung für die Aufnahmen im Kalksteinmassiv. In der Zusammenarbeit mit dem Photographen konnte ich alle Kapitelle vermessen und kurze Beschreibungen anfertigen.
Die Atmosphäre in den Gesprächen mit Ernest Will vor meiner Abreise nach Syrien 1974 war gut gewesen. Meine Pläne für die Untersuchung der Kapitelle

Das erste Projekt: Aufnahmen im Nordsyrischen Kalksteinmassiv

in den Siedlungen des Bergmassivs wurden positiv aufgenommen, und mein Arbeitsplan wurde weder zeitlich noch inhaltlich eingeschränkt. Dass es keine Einschränkungen gab, lag vielleicht daran, dass Ernest Will, ein hervorragender Klassischer Archäologe, die reichen Befunde zur Baudekoration im Kalksteinmassiv zu Beginn meiner Arbeiten nicht kannte.

Bei einem Treffen mit Henri Seyrig hatte Georges Tchalenko 1972 von meinen Projektplänen berichtet. Ich wurde von Seyrig zu einem Besuch eingeladen und fuhr darum im Oktober 1972 nach Neuchâtel, um mein Projekt vorzustellen. Henri Seyrig schilderte ausführlich und kritisch die Arbeitssituation im Kalksteinmassiv: Durch die Arbeiten von Georges Tchalenko waren die Orte des Bergmassivs französisches Konzessionsgebiet geworden (Taf. 37a). Ich nahm zur Kenntnis, dass diese Konzession nach der Ansicht von Seyrig und Tchalenko dringend geändert werden müsste. Ich sah sie aber damals nicht als Problem, da ich durch den Kontakt mit Tchalenko zu einer Arbeit an das französische Institut nach Syrien gekommen war.

Weitere Themen des Gesprächs in Neuchâtel waren die zweite große Publikation von Georges Tchalenko über die *„Églises syriennes à bêma"*, Kirchen mit einer besonderen liturgischen Einrichtung, dem Bema. Ich hatte vor meiner Reise nach Neuchâtel den gerade fertiggestellten Text in der Wohnung Tchalenkos gelesen und die größtenteils schon getuschten Zeichnungen sowie die für den dritten Band vorgesehenen Fotos gesehen. Henri Seyrig erwartete 1972 die baldige Publikation des Buches.

Bei der Aufnahme der Kirchen mit diesem liturgischen Mobiliar hatte Tchalenko auch die Kapitelle einzelner Bauten berücksichtigt. Es stand damit fest, dass ich mit den Arbeiten in Kirchen ohne Bema auf der einen und der Erforschung der von Tchalenko aufgenommenen Kapitelle auf der anderen Seite eng mit der Publikation der Bemakirchen verbunden sein würde.

1973. Neuorganisation der *Mission archéologique de Haute Syrie*; *„retraite"* von Tchalenko

Am 21. Januar 1973 starb überraschend Henri Seyrig. Georges Tchalenko hatte nicht nur einen langjährigen Freund, sondern auch seinen wichtigsten Förderer verloren. Auch nach Ablauf seiner Tätigkeit am Institut Français war Seyrig in ständigem Kontakt mit Tchalenko geblieben und hatte Kapitel für Kapitel die Arbeit am Bemabuch verfolgt.

Als Archäologin in Syrien

Die Schwierigkeiten, die unmittelbar nach dem Tod von Henri Seyrig einsetzten, hatten sich schon 1972 mit den Plänen für die Neuorganisation der Mission Archéologique der Haute Syrie angekündigt und steigerten sich bis zur Entlassung von Georges Tchalenko. Im Juni 1975 wurde ihm in offiziellem Schreiben mitgeteilt: Sein Vertrag mit dem Institut Français würde am 1. Oktober 1975 enden; bis dahin sei sein Archiv in das Institut zu überführen, und erst nach diesem Transfer würde ihm die finanzielle Abfindung nach 40 Jahren Arbeit ausgezahlt. Georges Tchalenko hatte als Staatenloser in der Kriegs- und Nachkriegszeit genug Schwierigkeiten gehabt. Erst 1963 hatte sich seine Situation durch Erhalt der libanesischen Staatsangehörigkeit etwas verbessert. Doch den Abtransport seines Archivs und damit auch seiner Zeichnungen und Fotos für die Publikation seines Buches hatte er nicht erwartet. Sein Kommentar lautete: *„Il est normal, qu´on veuille se débarasser de moi à mon age, mais il est annormal, que l´on veut me couper la possibilité de continuer mon oeuvre, en me privant de mes archives"* (Brief vom 10. Juni 1975). Helga Seeden von der American University in Beirut kommentierte brieflich die nachfolgende Situation: *„Nachdem alles auf einen großen Lastwagen verladen war, sah es in der Wohnung aus wie auf einem Schlachtfeld"*.

Edgar Baccache, über viele Jahre hin von Tchalenko als Zeichner ausgebildet, wurde mit anderen Aufgaben im Institut Français betraut: Damit hatte Tchalenko seinen letzten Mitarbeiter verloren. Das war eine Katastrophe für die druckreife Ausarbeitung der Originalzeichnungen des Buches und leider auch für die geplante Monographie der Kirche von Qalbloze.

Es war nicht der Bürgerkrieg im Libanon, der die Neuorganisation der Mission Archéologique de Haute Syrie verlangte, denn sie war schon 1972 geplant. Es ist aber nicht zu bezweifeln, dass der Tod von Henri Seyrig 1973 und die katastrophalen Ereignisse im Bürgerkrieg auf die dreizehn Jahre bis zum Tod Tchalenkos einwirkten. Ich berichte von diesen Ereignissen, weil sie auch meine Situation nach 1973 veränderten.

1974. Erste Kampagne im Kalksteinmassiv

Vor dem Rückflug von Helmut Loose im Juni 1974 fuhr ich mit ihm nach Bashmishli, das im Sommer mein Ausgangsort für die Arbeiten im Bergmassiv werden sollte. Die Reise mit Abu Feisal (Achmed Abd el Ghafour), dem Antikenwächter des Djebel Barisha und al-Ala, führte nach Qalbloze und Qirqbize (Taf. 3). Eine Asphaltstraße hinauf nach Qalbloze war im Bau. Ein Felsbrocken, deponiert am Straßenrand nach den Sprengungen, traf das Heck des VW-Busses bei der Abfahrt – ein gewaltiger Schlag. Das Auto schleuderte und mit viel Glück konnte ich am Steuer einen Sturz hinunter ins Tal vermeiden. Dies war das erste Ereignis, das mich unmittelbar zu Gertrude Bell und ihrem Bericht über den mehr als schwierigen Anstieg hinauf zur Basilika vor dem Bau der Straße erinnerte: Es war ein einziges Stolpern und Springen über Steinblöcke, immer in Gefahr, die Abhänge ins Tal hinab zu stürzen[12]. Genauso hatte ich meinen ersten Anstieg 1971 erlebt, und dennoch fragte ich mich, ob die Asphaltstraße wirklich eine Verbesserung brachte.

Im August 1974 brach ich erneut nach Bashmishli auf. Direkt neben dem Haus des Antikenwächters Abu Feisal hatte Georges Tchalenko einen kleinen einräumigen Bau errichtet, in dem er während seiner Arbeiten in den zentralen Regionen wohnte. Dieses Haus konnte ich mieten und es war mein kleines Paradies bei allen Arbeiten der Jahre 1974 und 1975 im Djebel Barisha und al-Ala. Die wunderbare Gastfreundschaft der Familie des Antikenwächters, seine Hilfe bei der Auswahl der Arbeiter und der Organisation von Mauleseln wie auch die rundherum freundliche Atmosphäre des ganzen Ortes prägen bis heute meine Erinnerungen an die ersten Jahre meiner Arbeit im Kalksteinmassiv.

An dieser Stelle komme ich noch einmal auf den Reisebericht von Gertrude Bell zurück: Sie war zu Pferd und teilweise zu Fuß im Bergmassiv unterwegs und baute die Zelte der Route folgend auf. Wichtiger als alles andere waren ihr die Kontakte zu allen Schichten der syrischen Bevölkerung. Ihre überragenden Kenntnisse der arabischen Sprache ermöglichte jedes Gespräch über Alltagsfragen wie auch über politische Themen. Meine Kenntnis des Arabischen reichte leider nur für kurze Gespräche bei Familienbesuchen oder offiziellen Treffen und vor allem für Gespräche mit den Arbeitern, die mich begleiteten. Ich hatte in jeder Region einen zentralen Wohnort, von dem aus die Arbeiten in anderen Orten organisiert wurde. Vor allem aber waren meine Aufenthalte bestimmt von intensiver Arbeit in jeweils ein oder zwei Bauten des Zielortes und nur kurzer Vorstellung bei den Ältesten jedes Ortes direkt nach der Ankunft unserer kleinen Gruppe.

Trotz dieser Unterschiede war mir der Bericht von Gertrude Bell mehr als nur vertraut, da sich zu meiner Zeit die Situation im Kalksteinmassiv nur geringfügig verändert hatte. Die Ruinenorte mit ihren Oliven- und Feigenbäumen, kleinen Tabak- und Getreidefeldern hatten mich verzaubert, waren zu Orten der Sehnsucht geworden. Alles so kristallklar als gäbe es gar keinen Staub, jede Kerbe im bläulichen Kalkstein so frisch, als wäre sie erst gestern entstanden und bereit, unzählige kleine Blüten aufzunehmen (Taf. 5a. b).

Beim ersten Hahnenschrei ging es hinaus in den Olivenhain, wo ich mit der Klopapierrolle unter dem Arm und einer Plastikflasche mit Wasser den mir zugewiesenen Baum als morgendliche Toilette aufsuchte – mein Darm brauchte einige Zeit, um sich an diesen Ritus zu gewöhnen. Nach dem Frühstück mit Tee, knusprig-frischem Fladenbrot, eingelegtem Käse, Oliven und Joghurt wurden die Maulesel beladen: meine Fotokoffer, die großen Fotokartons, einige Werkzeuge, große Wasserflaschen und das Essen für die Arbeiter, den Antikenwächter Abu Feisal und mich. Für den Fußmarsch zu den einzelnen antiken Orten waren die Stunden vor 8 Uhr zu nutzen, denn schon gegen 9 Uhr setzte die Hitze ein.

Meine Arbeit begann in jeder Kirche mit einem Plan, der die Lage der einzelnen Kapitelle und weiterer Elemente der Baudekoration festhielt. Die meisten Kapitelle konnten in dem Versturz der Kalksteinquader leicht ausgemacht werden, da sie nicht von Erd- oder Sandverwehungen bedeckt waren. Die Arbeiter konnten die von Quadern teilweise verdeckten Kapitelle soweit freilegen und mit Holzbalken abstützen, dass sie von mir vermessen und für Fotos bewegt werden konnten. In der Mittagspause bereitete ich die Arbeiten für den Nachmittag vor und versuchte, mir einen Überblick über den jeweiligen Ort und seine Bauten zu verschaffen. Die Arbeiten konnten in der Regel nicht an einem Tag abgeschlossen werden, da zu ihrem Abschluss auch die Wiederherstellung der ursprünglichen Fundsituation der Kapitelle und eine Beschreibung der Türen und Fassadengestaltung jeder Kirche gehörte. So wurde häufig der Ort des Vortags auf dem Weg zu dem neuen Ort noch einmal aufgesucht. Mühselig war immer der Rückweg mit den müden, vom Rauf und Runter in den Quaderbergen erschöpften Beinen.

Die Organisation der Reise von Gertrude Bell hatte mit den Zelten und häufigen Ortswechseln weitgehend der des Teams der Princeton Expedition entsprochen. Ich erreichte mit meinem kleinen Team die einzelnen Orte erst nach langen Fußmärschen – in der Regel 10–15 und manchmal sogar 20–30 km Hin- und Rückweg pro Tag. Doch erlebte auch ich die Kulturlandschaft des nordsyrischen Kalksteinmassivs ohne Asphaltstraßen, auf kleinen Bergpisten und durch innere Ebenen (Taf. 5a). Nichts hat das Bergmassiv so tiefgreifend verändert wie der Bau zahlreicher Asphaltstraßen in den 80er Jahren des 20. Jahrhunderts – darauf werde ich später zurückkommen.

Das erste Projekt: Aufnahmen im Nordsyrischen Kalksteinmassiv

Bei den erwähnten Treffen mit den Ältesten eines Dorfes konnte ich nach Austausch von Höflichkeiten Gespräche über die Familie, eventuelle Krankheiten und benötigte Medizin führen. Bei allen Aufenthalten nach 1974 nahm ich dann als erwünschte Gastgeschenke aus Deutschland so viele Aspirintabletten wie möglich, englische Fruchtbonbons in der Dose, Taschenlampen, Sonnenbrillen und kleine Ferngläser mit. Im Zusammensein mit den Arbeitern vergrößerte sich mein Wortschatz von Jahr zu Jahr. Das wunderte mich, da ich mit Kurden, Turkmenen und Drusen arbeitete und ein wahres Durcheinander von Begriffen (dabei auch erstaunlich viele Schimpfwörter) in meinem Gehirn versenkte.

Die Kampagne der Monate August und September führte zu insgesamt 28 Orten im Djebel al-Ala und Djebel Simʿan (Taf. 2. 3) und nach jeder Woche einmal nach Aleppo zum Einkauf von Mineralwasser, Kaffeebohnen für Umm Feisal, Oliven, Käse etc. Bei der Arbeit in den einzelnen Orten konnte ich auf den Ergebnissen der „*Eglises syriennes à bêma*" aufbauen. Das heißt, ich ergänzte in den Bemakirchen die Kapitellaufnahmen von Tchalenko und konzentrierte mich bei neuen Aufnahmen ganz auf die Baudekoration der Kirchen ohne Bema und erweiterte sie durch Aufnahmen in einzelnen Hausbauten. In zahlreichen Orten waren zwei oder drei Kirchen mit höchst gegensätzlichen Kapitell- und Türformen erhalten. Schon früh warfen die großen Unterschiede zwischen den einzelnen Kirchenbauten die Frage auf, ob sie allein auf Gegensätze innerhalb der Werkstätten / Werkgruppen oder auf Einflüsse aus dem städtischen Bereich zurückgingen.

So stieß ich in der zu jeder Zeit bewunderten Weitarkadenbasilika von Qalbloze – dem Lieblingsbau von Georges Tchalenko – zum ersten Mal auf ein äußerst vielschichtiges Gesamtbild der Baudekoration, das mit seinen so unterschiedlichen Formen von Kapitellen, Türen und Gesimsen das Miteinander verschiedener Werkgruppen vor Augen führte[13]. Die Frage war: Welche Werkleute kamen aus dem Bergmassiv und welche waren eventuell von außen, aus einer der großen Städte gekommen oder nahmen dort ausgebildete Formen auf?

Im September traf ich in Aleppo im Hotel Baron auf Georges Tchalenko und Jean-Pierre Sodini mit seinem Architekten Jean-Luc Biscop: Die Aufnahme von Deḥes als herausragendes Projekt des Institut Français wurde für das Jahr 1975 vorbereitet und man wartete auf Georges Tate, d. h. auf den Abschluss seines Studiums in Frankreich.

Als Archäologin in Syrien

Anfang Oktober fuhr ich nach Qalʿat Simʿan und blieb dort, nach kurzem Zwischenaufenthalt in Damaskus, bis Ende November. Ich wohnte in dem kleinen Haus, das Tchalenko vor der Nordwestecke der kreuzförmigen Anlage errichtet hatte: Eine kleine Holztür führte auf eine lange, überdeckte Terrasse, die sich in zwei Räume mit einfacher Einrichtung öffnete[14]. In diesem kleinen Haus mit dem Blick hinunter in die Ebene von Afrin und weitem Blick bis in die Türkei erlebte ich die schönste Zeit meiner Jahre in Syrien.

Nach so viel positiver Schilderung ist an dieser Stelle wohl doch ein Kommentar fällig zur oft gestellten Frage: Hatten Sie denn keine Probleme als europäische Frau? Ich hatte – im Gegensatz zu meinen Erfahrungen in Deutschland – in Syrien keine Probleme und es war Mustafa, der Wächter in Qalʿat Simʿan dessen Erklärung ich hier weitergebe: *„Sie haben ein Auto, Fotoapparate, Geld um die Arbeiter zu bezahlen: Sie sind reich"*. Und dann folgte noch eine etwas vorsichtige Beschreibung meiner Erscheinung (1,80 m Körpergröße), die doch eher an Frauengestalten aus alten Sagen erinnere. Was er damit meinte, blieb bei allen Rückfragen unklar. Da Eva Strommenger vergleichbar positive Erfahrungen gemacht hat, sei hier ihre Erklärung im Anschluss an einige negative Erfahrungen in Deutschland zitiert: *„Eine derartige Diskriminierung wie diese in meinem Heimatland musste ich anderswo niemals erleiden. Insbesondere im Rahmen meiner Tätigkeit im Irak und in Syrien wurde mein Einsatz stets anerkannt"* [15].

Meine Aufgabe in Qalʿat Simʿan war die detaillierte Aufnahme der Kapitelle in den vier Kreuzarmen (Taf. 6), und ich wurde gastfreundlich aufgenommen und von fünf Arbeitern unterstützt, wo immer es erforderlich war. Die Älteren in Deir Simʿan erinnerten sich noch an die Jahre, in denen sie bei der Restaurierung in Qalʿat Simʿan unter Tchalenko mitgearbeitet hatten. Es war vor allem die Familie des kurdischen *Muchtars* von Deir Simʿan, Beschir Abd el Kadr, in deren Kreis ich viele Stunden verbrachte. Sie verwöhnte mich auf alle erdenkliche Weise: Frühmorgens stand vor der Eingangstür in mein kleines Paradies ein Korb mit Oliven, Paprika, Joghurt, Käse, Eiern, Granatäpfeln aus Dana und manchmal sogar Honig.

Damals gelangten nur wenige Touristen nach Qalʿat Simʿan. Der steile Weg hinauf zum Osteingang war noch nicht asphaltiert, das Restaurant vor der Nordseite war noch nicht erbaut und der Ort gehörte noch nicht zum Ausflugsprogramm syrischer Schulen. Kamen wir ohne Auto, so gingen wir den alten Pilgerweg der Westseite, hinauf zum Plateau (Taf. 6b) und zu der noch nicht verbauten Nordseite des Pilgerzentrums (Taf. 6a. 11a). Was für ein Unterschied zu der turbulenten Situation, die ich in späteren Jahrzehnten antraf!

Im November setzten die Winterstürme ein. Mustafa, der Wächter von Qalʿat Simʿan, hatte auf der Innenseite von Süd- und Westarm der kreuzförmigen Anlage, also vor den großen Öffnungen, durch die der Wind fegte, ein Seil gespannt, an dem entlang ich sicher mein Häuschen erreichen konnte. Wie, um Himmels willen, hatte sich Simeon hoch oben auf seiner Säule halten können, ohne sich anzuseilen – der interessierte Leser lese die syrische Vita.

Ende Oktober war Besuchszeit in meinem Schlösschen: Zuerst kam Georges Tchalenko für zwei Tage und zu langen Gesprächen über seine Arbeiten in den 30er und 40er Jahren in Qalʿat Simʿan. Besonders faszinierend war sein Bericht über die Restaurierung der Eingangsanlage des südlichen Arms der kreuzförmigen Anlage (Taf. 11b). Dann kamen die Mitarbeiter von Eva Strommengers Grabung in Habuba Kabira zum Gegenbesuch – ich hatte im September deren Grabung besichtigt. Sie hatten in Aleppo allerlei seltsame europäische Gerichte in Dosen (Wursti con Krauti!) und mehrere Flaschen Liebfrauenmilch eingekauft. Alles wurde zum Kühlen in die Zisterne an der Simeonssäule hinabgelassen (Taf. 14b) und dann für ein 5-Sterne-Menü wieder hochgeholt. Zum Glück hatten alle Luftmatratzen mit...

Während meiner ersten Aufnahmen der Kapitelle in den vier Kreuzarmen hatte ich erkannt, dass ich mit ihrer Analyse nur einen Teil der vielfachen, mit dem außerordentlich reichen Befund der Baudekoration verbundenen Fragen erfassen konnte. Einige der Kapitell-, Tür- und Gesimsformen hatte ich bei meinen Arbeiten in den drei Regionen des Kalksteinmassivs angetroffen. In einigen Kirchen des 6. Jahrhunderts führte der Befund in Einzelformen aber über Qalʿat Simʿan hinaus und in wiederum einer ganzen Anzahl von Bauten unterschied sich das Gesamtbild grundlegend von dem des Pilgerzentrums Qalʿat Simʿan. Mein erster Eindruck war, dass ich in dem breit aufgefächerten Befund der Orte des Kalksteinmassivs einmal eine Situation vor und ein andermal eine nach der Errichtung der Anlage von Qalʿat Simʿan vor Augen hatte. Darum wurde für mich – trotz der Konzentration auf Säulen- und Pfeilerkapitelle – die zumindest beschreibende Erfassung des Gesamtbildes der Baudekoration in jedem einzelnen Bau grundlegend wichtig.

Wie wurde das große Zentrum (Taf. 11a. 14b) in vorangegangenen Jahrzehnten beurteilt? Howard Crosby Butler stellte 1929 fest: *„If we could but recover a few fragments of the Christian architecture of Antioch, we should probably find* *that the church of Saint Simeon was only a reflection of the architecture of the capital city*" ¹⁶. Georges Tchalenko ging als erster auf Grundzüge der Baudekoration ein und sah neben lokalen eine Fülle importierter Elemente „*tant syriens qu'étrangers*", und nannte an erster Stelle die Beteiligung von lokalen Werkgruppen¹⁷. Alle Autoren, die wie Gertrude Bell die enge Bindung der Architektur und Baudekoration an die Metropole Antiochia vermuteten, konnten keinen der Sakralbauten Antiochias zum Vergleich heranziehen, da von hunderten überlieferten Kirchen keine innerhalb der Stadt erhalten oder, aufgrund der tiefen Verschüttung, bei Grabungen zutage gekommen war.

Es blieb nur ein Weg, um Antworten zu finden: Umfangreiche Aufnahmen der Baudekoration in allen Regionen des Bergmassivs, um die Tradition lokaler Werkgruppen von denen der Städte, in deren Einflussbereich es liegt, zu trennen.

Da saß ich also auf dem Sockel der Säule des Simeon (Taf. 14b) und suchte nach einer Lösung aus einem Dilemma: Ich hatte mit der Konzession für die Aufnahme der Kapitelle einen Weg gefunden, für ein neues Projekt in das Bergmassiv zu gehen. Innerhalb einer Werkgruppe oder Werkstatt wurde die Ausarbeitung eines Kapitells in der Regel den am besten geschulten Steinmetzen übertragen. In den Säulenkapitellen sind also ländliche Traditionen und darüber hinausführende, aus dem städtischen Bereich kommende Neuerungen besonders gut greifbar.

Ich hatte aber in den vergangenen Monaten begriffen, dass die Kapitelle als Teil des Gesamtbildes der Baudekoration jedes einzelnen Baus zu betrachten sind. Erst dieses Gesamtbild würde den Charakter einzelner Werkgruppen / Werkstätten greifbar machen. Würde ich in den kommenden Kampagnen in der Lage sein, neben den Kapitellen auch den Befund von Türen und Gesimsen wenigstens beschreibend zu erfassen? Und würde ich wenigsten einige besonders aussagekräftige Stücke in Auswahl in meine Publikation aufnehmen können?

Nach Abschluss der ersten Kampagne schickte ich von Qalʿat Simʿan aus meinen Bericht über alle Aktivitäten der ersten Kampagne an Afif Bachnassi, den Generaldirektor der Syrischen Antikenkommission in Damaskus und stellte den Antrag für eine zweite Kampagne im Jahr 1975.

Am 27. November nahm ich wehmütig Abschied, fuhr nach Beirut, brachte das Auto und mich auf das Schiff und fuhr nach Venedig. Es half mir nichts, dass ich in Brixen am 2. Dezember vor der Weiterfahrt nach München übernachtet hatte, denn nach der Auffahrt auf die Brennerautobahn fuhr ein bei Glatteis schleudernder italienischer Lastwagen am 3. Dezember mein Auto zu Schrott und ich landete nicht in München, sondern im Krankenhaus in Innsbruck und erst nach zwei Wochen im Krankenhaus in München.

1975. Beginn des Bürgerkriegs; zweite Kampagne im Kalksteinmassiv

Im Frühjahr bearbeitete ich in München die Materialaufnahmen der ersten Kampagne und erholte mich langsam von den Folgen des Unfalls. Die Lähmung der linken Gesichtshälfte ging langsam zurück und ebenso die Störung des Gleichgewichts. Die gebrochenen Fußzehen heilten langsam, doch ein Bruch des Felsenbeins hatte mein rechtes Ohr für immer schwer beschädigt. Die beste Nachricht bei meinen Vorbereitungen für den Sommer war, dass der inzwischen diplomierte Architekt Alexander Wetzig, der schon 1971 mitgereist war, an der geplanten Kampagne teilnehmen würde.

In die Vorbereitungszeit fielen einige der Ereignisse, die zum Beginn des Bürgerkriegs im Libanon führten: In dem Angriff auf eine Kirche am 3. April 1975 und der nachfolgenden Rache christlicher Milizen, die daraufhin 27 Insassen eines Busses – die meisten Palästinenser – töteten, wird im Rückblick einer der Vorfälle gesehen, die den Beginn des Bürgerkrieges im Libanon auslösten. In dem monatelangen Briefwechsel zwischen Ernest Will, Georges Tchalenko und Klaus Wessel, der als Institutschef in München mein Stipendium betreute, ist von diesen Ereignissen, die die Situation in Beirut tiefgreifend veränderten und in der Folgezeit zur Aufgabe des dortigen Institut Français sowie zur Übertragung der Bibliothek an das Institut Français in Damaskus führten, nichts zu spüren.

Der umfangreiche Briefwechsel betraf ausschließlich die Forderung einer Gruppe in Paris, alle Fotos, die mir Tchalenko nach der Reise mit seinem Mitarbeiter Claude Vernet 1971 gegeben hatte, sowie alle Kopien von Zeichnungen seines Archivs, die in meinem Besitz seien, zurückzugeben. Die Fotos von Claude Vernet wollte ich nicht haben, denn sie waren fast durchgehend missglückt. Ich hatte dagegen bereits 1972 meine circa 3000 Fotos in 13×18-Vergrößerungen an Tchalenko geschickt. Es ging also um die Zeichnungen und Fotos für das Bemabuch. Es war kein Geheimnis, dass ich schon 1971 das Manuskript des Bemabuches gelesen und 1975 eine Kopie des Textes sowie einiger Zeichnungen erhalten hatte. In meinen Briefen an Ernest Will 1975 hatte ich gedankt, dass ich bei meiner ersten Kampagne auf den Ergebnissen zu den „*Églises syriennes*" aufbauen und mich auf die Baudekoration der Kirchen ohne Bema konzentrieren konnte. Warum also nach zwei Jahren diese Reaktion aus Paris?

Es ist traurig, von der Kette deprimierender Ereignisse in den letzten Lebensjahren Georges Tchalenkos zu berichten. In meinen Nachruf (1989) und in meine Rezension zu den „*Églises syriennes à bêma*" (1992) sind schon einige Informationen eingegangen[18]. Doch erst in diesem Bericht kann ich darstellen, wie sehr meine erste Projektplanung und meine folgende Arbeit im Kalksteinmassiv mit der Mission Archéologique de Haute Syrie und Ereignissen im Libanon und in Syrien verflochten waren.

Eine positive Entwicklung ist zu erwähnen, die während der zweiten Kampagne eintrat: 1975 wurde Kassem Toueir Direktor des Département de recherches archéologiques an der Generaldirektion in Damaskus. Mit seiner umfassenden Kenntnis der frühbyzantinischen und frühislamischen Zeit wurde er mein wichtigster Ratgeber in den folgenden Jahren.

Im Mittelpunkt der Kampagne im Jahr 1975 standen die Siedlungen des Djebel Zawiye (Taf. 3). Diese südliche Region hatte ich 1974 nicht aufgesucht, hatte jedoch bei der Reise von 1971 einige seiner Orte flüchtig kennengelernt. Schon der erste Eindruck ließ damals deutliche Unterschiede der Architektur von Haus- und Kirchenbauten der Apamene wie auch ihrer Baudekoration zu den zentralen und nördlichen Regionen des Kalksteinmassivs, der Antiochene, erkennen – an der Spitze des Arbeitsprogramms stand deshalb ein langer Aufenthalt in El Bara, der bedeutendsten Siedlung der Region[19].

In El Bara wurde das Haus des Antikenwächters Abu Aboud das Hauptquartier von Alexander Wetzig und mir. Es lag in der neuzeitlichen Siedlung, die gegenüber dem antiken Ort errichtet worden war (Taf. 7a). Eine ganz spezielle Situation verband beide Orte: Das Terrain jeder der zahlreichen Kirchen war im Besitz einer Familie. Niedrige Mauern aus Feldsteinen fassten jeden Besitz ein und machten jeden Gang durch die antike Siedlung zu einer ermüdenden Kletterpartie über Mäuerchen.

Nach der Ankunft am 1. September und der Organisation einer kleinen Gruppe von Arbeitern brachen wir schon am nächsten Tag nach Deir Sambul auf. Selten traf ich in einem Ruinenort auf so glänzend erhaltene, reich ausgestattete Häuser. Auch der Anblick der Kirche war ein Erlebnis: Ost- und Westseite hoch anstehend und glänzend erhaltene Säulenkapitelle mit windbewegtem Akanthus

Das erste Projekt: Aufnahmen im Nordsyrischen Kalksteinmassiv

in Fundlage (Taf. 7b). Mit der hohen Qualität der Baudekoration und mit dem gerissenen Drahtseil neben einem Kapitell, dessen Deckplatte für den Abtransport tief eingekerbt war, führte Deir Sambul in zweifacher Hinsicht in die Situation ein, die uns im Djebel Zawiye erwartete: windbewegte Kapitelle sowohl in Kirchen wie in Häusern. Unter ihnen gab es perfekt ausgearbeitete Kapitelle aus den Jahren vor Qalʿat Simʿan, doch waren sie gefährdet durch Antikenraub in Orten, die mit dem Pickup erreichbar waren. Ich erkannte, dass die große Anzahl von Hauskapitellen dieses Typus, die ich in der Sammlung Pharaon angetroffen hatte, aus dem Djebel Zawiye stammte (Taf. 4b).

Leider muss ich gleich zu Beginn unserer Arbeiten in El Bara die Situation im dortigen Wächterhaus ansprechen, die uns den Ort nicht zu der „*Zauberstadt*" machte, die Gertrude Bell so begeistert beschrieben hatte. Wir waren gerade auf dem Weg nach Shinsharah, das mich 1971 so beeindruckt hatte, als mich der Onkel von Abu Aboud (Taf. 37b) vorwarnte: „*Seien Sie nicht enttäuscht; alle Kapitelle der Kirche sind weg*". Ich kam an, sah das Durcheinander im Kircheninneren mit dem Rest von ehemals neun Kapitellen und explodierte. Die Arbeiter waren, wie man mir sagte, beeindruckt und sehr arbeitswillig in den folgenden Tagen.

Den Abtransport der Kapitelle hatte Abu Aboud organisiert, und es dauerte nicht lange um zu realisieren, dass Antikenraub sein Spezialgebiet war. Vollkommen anders war damals die Haltung von Abu Feisal in Bashmishli (Taf. 37b), der „*seine Orte*" liebte und darunter litt, dass er kein Moped besaß, das es ihm leichter gemacht hätte, die Situation in seinen Orten zu kontrollieren.

Wir haben alle Orte des Djebel Zawiye aufgesucht (Taf. 3): Nur Djerade und Ruweiha besaßen eine Kirche mit Bema, die von Georges Tchalenko detailliert aufgenommen worden war. Die Ausgangssituation unserer Arbeiten war also grundlegend anders als in der Antiochene. Im Zentrum standen über Wochen die Kirchen El Baras, für die Tchalenko als Erster Grundrisse erarbeitet und Teilaufnahmen angefertigt hatte.

Bei jeder der fünf Hauptkirchen, fast alle Emporenkirchen, standen wir vor einer ganz speziellen Situation:

a) Das Zentrum der Kirche *extra muros* (El Hosn) war für die Anlage eines Feldes ausgeräumt worden und alle erhaltenen Elemente des Baus bildeten hohe seitliche Schuttberge.

b) In der Hauptkirche des 5. Jahrhunderts mit den gewaltigen Versturzlagen ihrer beiden Geschosse waren die Kapitelle der obersten Fundlagen ausgeraubt, tief verschüttete dagegen erhalten. Die Hauptüren der Westseite, berühmt durch die Zeichnungen Melchior de Vogüés[20], waren eingestürzt.

c) Der Befund der Transeptkirche hatte, trotz des gut erhaltenen Ostteils, am meisten gelitten: Der Innenraum war weitgehend leergeräumt, Tür- und Gesimsfragmente in den eingrenzenden Mauern des Terrains verbaut und einige besonders aufwendige Kapitelle in Häusern der neuzeitlichen Siedlung wiederverwandt worden.

d) In der kleinen Kirche des 6. Jahrhunderts waren zwar auch die obersten Kapitelle verschwunden, doch sie war als Bau sehr gut erhalten.

Es stellte sich schnell heraus, dass ich einige Kapitelle der El Hosn in der Sammlung Pharaon vorgefunden und aufgenommen hatte. Dies wiederholte sich bei zwei Kapitellen der Transeptkirche (Taf. 4a). Hinzu kam, dass auch die Kapitelle, deren Fotos Georges Tchalenko mir zur Überprüfung mitgegeben hatte, verschwunden waren. Dies ließ nicht daran zweifeln, dass Aufnahmen in jeder Kirche dringend notwendig waren. Wir arbeiteten mit einer ganz besonders starken Motivation, das heißt, mit dem Wissen, dass wir nicht sicher sein konnten, bei unserer nächsten Kampagne die aufgenommenen Kapitelle wieder vorzufinden. Wir fertigten Fundpläne der großen Kirchen an, nahmen einige Kapitelle detailliert und andere, tief verschüttete, in Hauptmaßen auf, fotografierten die Bauelemente, die für die Rekonstruktion des Gesamtbildes wichtig zu sein schienen und hatten doch das Gefühl, das dies alles zu wenig war. Vor allem die Arbeiten in der Transeptkirche mussten leider auf eine spätere Kampagne verschoben werden.

In Anschluss an die Aufnahmen in El Bara fuhren wir nach Apamea (Taf. 2. 3), der ‚Hauptstadt' der Apamene, wo wir leider nur wenige Kapitelle vorfanden, die in den Djebel Zawiye zurückführten. Jahrzehntelanger Antikenraub hatte auch hier vor allem die Kapitelle getroffen. Wieder konnte ich wenigstens einige Kapitelle der Sammlung Pharaon nach Apamea zurückverfolgen. Nach erholsamen Tagen im Haus der belgischen Grabung, fruchtbaren Gesprächen mit unseren Freunden Jean und Janine Balty, die seit 1965 die Grabung leiteten und unsere Probleme bei den Arbeiten im Kalksteinmassiv nur zu gut nachvollzie-

Das erste Projekt: Aufnahmen im Nordsyrischen Kalksteinmassiv

hen konnten, brachen wir nach Aleppo auf. Die Fortsetzung der Aufnahmen in Orten der Antiochene wurde vorbereitet.

Die Wochen im Haus von Abu Feisal, die insgesamt harmonische Atmosphäre in Bashmishli – nach der Zeit in El Bara haben wir alles doppelt genossen. In den ersten Tagen kamen Alexander Wetzig und ich – unterstützt von Abu Feisal und vier Arbeitern – zu ergänzenden Aufnahmen nach Bakirha, Dar Qita, Behyo und Bettir. Danach begannen die Erstaufnahmen in Bankusa, Deir Seta, Kaukanaya, Djuwaniye, Meʿez und Bafetin (Taf. 3). Schwerpunkt aller Aufnahmen war die Kapitellplastik der Kirchen des 6. Jahrhunderts, die, wie schon 1974, durch Aufnahmen in einzelnen Hausbauten erweitert wurde. Auch in dieser Kampagne zeichnete sich klar ab, dass ergänzende Aufnahmen in einer weiteren Kampagne absolut notwendig sein würden.

Nach dem Rückflug von Alexander Wetzig ging ich im Oktober noch einmal für zwei Wochen nach Qalʿat Simʿan und Deir Simʿan. Bei meinem abschließenden Aufenthalt in Aleppo schickte ich den Bericht über meine Aktivitäten nach Damaskus an die Syrische Antikenkommission, stellte bei meinem Treffen mit dem Direktor des Museums in Aleppo die Ergebnisse der beiden Kampagnen vor und informierte ihn, dass ich in Damaskus und am Institut Français den Antrag auf eine weitere Kampagne im Jahr 1977 stellen würde. Ich war dankbar für die gute Atmosphäre der Gespräche in Aleppo.

Fahrt nach Izmir

Die Rückfahrt mit dem Schiff war ab Beirut geplant, doch ein Anruf im Hotel Ramsis aus dem Deutschen Orientinstitut in Beirut an meinem letzten Tag in Aleppo änderte alles: Die Situation in Beirut hatte sich erheblich verschärft – heftige Kämpfe in der Stadt, große Probleme am Hafen. Es wurde mir geraten, von Izmir aus mit der Turkish Maritime Line zurückzufahren. Ich machte mich sofort auf zur syrischen Grenze und landete an der Grenzstation Bab al-Hawa in einem riesigen Stau von Autos: In der Türkei war Volkszähltag, *census*. Ich kann nicht mehr rekonstruieren, was ich bei meinen dramatischen Schilderungen an der Grenze und meinen Anrufen beim Gouverneur in Ishkenderun erzählte, doch das Wunder geschah: Ich erhielt die Konzession zur Weiterfahrt nach Izmir und fuhr mit einem großen Schreiben an der Windschutzscheibe bei herrlichem Herbstwetter auf leeren, autofreien Straßen nach Izmir.

Als ich dort ankam und mein Auto im Atatürk-Boulevard abstellte, sah ich direkt gegenüber von meinem Auto einen Buchladen und trat ein. Nach der Auswahl von zwei Büchern ging ich zur Kasse, sah auf die hoch erhobene Titelseite der FAZ *„Beirut in Flammen"* und fing an zu lesen. Die FAZ sank herab und lächelnd fragte mich die Dame an der Kasse: *„Wo kommen Sie denn her?"* Ich zeigte auf den Titel. Mit lautem Ruf wurde Harry Blackburn an die Kasse gebeten und es war Elisabeth Blackburn – wie ich bald erfuhr –, die klipp und klar feststellte, dass ich sie für ein warmes Bad und einen guten Tee zu ihrer nahegelegenen Wohnung zu begleiten hatte. Ich folgte, genoss alsbald ein warmes Bad, der Teewagen rollte herein und ich grübelte, wie abgehalftert ich wohl ausgesehen hatte, als ich an der Kasse stand. Am Abend wurden Freunde von Harry und Elisabeth Blackburn eingeladen, ich hatte so viel wie möglich vom Libanon zu berichten. Die Mitbringsel aus meinem Bus wurden ausgepackt und herumgereicht. Am Höhepunkt des Abends entdeckten der Baron von Angeli und ich eine uns gemeinsame Leidenschaft: das Basteln von Ketten aus Perlen und Silberkugeln – was für ein Tag.

Am Tag der Abfahrt mit der Turkish Maritime Line begleiteten mich alle zum Hafen. Ich stand auf dem Deck und wurde von hinten angetippt: *„Dreh dich mal um"*. Es war das Team der Pergamongrabung, das ebenfalls das letzte Schiff gebucht hatte. Auf der Rückreise wurde viel von Elisabeth Blackburn erzählt, die allen Mitarbeitern der deutschen Grabungen bekannt war. Dankbar genoss ich das kleine Buch von Enno Littmann über die Geschichte *„Vom Morgenländischen Floh"* das sie mir geschenkt hatte. Die Reise nach München nach der Ankunft in Venedig verlief ausnahmsweise einmal ohne Unfall.

1976. Aufenthalt in Rom. Auswertung der Arbeitskampagnen

Anfang 1976 führ ich an das Deutsche Archäologische Institut in Rom, dessen Bibliothek die besten Bedingungen für die Ausarbeitung der Aufnahmen in Syrien bot. Ich wohnte in der Altstadt und genoss ein ganzes Jahr das erholsame und lebensfrohe Ambiente in Rom nach anstrengender Arbeit. Im Dezember ging ich mit dem fertigen Text- und Tafelband nach München zurück, reichte die Arbeit zur Habilitation an der Universität ein und stellte bei der Deutschen Forschungsgemeinschaft einen Antrag auf Fortsetzung der Aufnahmen in Syrien bei der. Dem Antrag war ein Briefwechsel mit dem Institut Français in Beirut und der Syrischen Antikenkommission in Damaskus vorangegangen, der mir grünes Licht für eine weitere Kampagne gegeben hatte.

Das erste Projekt: Aufnahmen im Nordsyrischen Kalksteinmassiv

1977. Dritte Kampagne im Kalksteinmassiv

Nach Abschluss der Habilitation im Sommer 1977 und Bewilligung einer Sachbeihilfe der Deutschen Forschungsgemeinschaft, angeschlossen an das Institut für Byzantinistik in München, begann ich die Vorbereitung der dritten Kampagne in Syrien. Die bessere finanzielle Ausstattung ermöglichte die Einstellung der Architektin Ulrike Hess für die ganze Kampagne und die zusätzliche Einstellung des Architekten Thomas Rhode für drei Wochen (Taf. 37c). Die Aufnahmen mit 6×6- und Kleinbildkameras sowie die Vermessung der Kapitelle und Aufnahme der Fundlagen sollten wie bei den vorangegangenen Arbeiten in meiner Hand, die zeichnerischen Aufnahmen ausgewählter Tür- und Gesimsformen in den Händen der Architekten sein.

Wieder wurde das Haus von Abu Feisal im August und September für einige Wochen unser Hauptsitz. Wir begannen mit ergänzenden Aufnahmen in Qalbloze, Bettir und Behyo und gingen dann zu detaillierten Aufnahmen in den Kirchen des 6. Jahrhunderts nach Kefr Kila, Barisha, Bafetin, Meʿez, Kaukanaya, Djuwaniye, Deir Seta, Bankusa, Bakirha und Dar Qita (Taf. 3). Triste Erfahrungen mit Antikenraub machten wir nur in den wenigen Orten, die mit dem Pickup erreichbar waren.

Die so eindrucksvolle, in einer Ebene gelegene Siedlung Meʿez hatte es schon vor 1971 hart getroffen: Von den reichen Kapitellen der Kirche des 6. Jahrhunderts, die Georges Tchalenko in den 50er Jahren aufgenommen hatte, waren nur noch vereinzelte kleine Fragmente am Ort. Bei der großartigen Kirche im leicht erreichbaren Ort Deir Seta waren die noch gegen 1900 vorhandenen Kapitelle verschwunden, doch mit einigen Fragmenten konnte das Gesamtbild rekonstruiert werden. Im schwerer erreichbaren Bankusa war der Versturz des Innenraums fast ungestört, doch in der großen Kirche von Bafetin läuteten beim Anblick kleiner Splitter eines für den Abtransport in zwei Teile zerschlagenen Kapitells die Alarmglocken.

Bei den sporadischen Aufenthalten in Aleppo waren wir nach dem Besitzerwechsel im Hotel Baron in das Hotel Ramsis umgezogen und sahen dort nicht nur das Grabungsteam aus Habuba Kabira wieder, sondern trafen auch mit Landsleuten aus der DDR zusammen. Ich erinnere mich besonders an ihre Berichte über die gerade in Syrien errichteten Hühnerfarmen und Getreidesilos. Die Kontakte der DDR-Regierung nach Damaskus führten bis in die 60er Jahre zurück und prägten auch die Situation an der Generaldirektion der Altertümer und Museen: Ab und zu folgte auf einen in Paris promovierten ein Generaldirektor mit Studium und Promotion in Westberlin oder in der DDR.

In den letzten Tagen des Fastenmonats Ramadan fuhren die beiden Architekten nach Raqqa, Palmyra, Habuba Kabira und ich allein mit dem VW-Bus nach Beirut. Zu viele Fragen konnten per Post oder Telefon nicht mehr geklärt werden, und ich brauchte dringend Informationen über die Situation von Georges Tchalenko nach seiner „*retraite*". Vom ersten bis zum letzten Tag waren die Tage in Beirut trostlos und zutiefst belastend. Nach endlosen Schikanen an der libanesischen Grenzstation, kam ich auf der Autobahn Damaskus-Aleppo hinter Homs in die Dunkelheit – eine Situation, die wir, wenn möglich, immer vermieden.

Nach einem Unfall, Transport in das Gefängnis von Hama

Zum Glück fuhr ich aufgrund der starken Windböen zwischen Homs und Hama langsam, als ein Dreirad ohne Beleuchtung aus dem Graben neben der Autobahn auftauchte und in die Front meines Busses krachte. Die beiden Bauern flogen zurück in den Acker, ich befreite mich aus den Scherben der Frontscheibe, aus Tomaten und Kartoffeln und stand in einer Menschengruppe, die aus dem Nichts aufgetaucht war. Die beiden Fahrer kamen ins Krankenhaus und ich ins Gefängnis von Hama. Es stellte sich heraus, dass sie, oh Wunder, nur leichte Schürfungen und Prellungen hatten und der junge Arzt im Krankenhaus verhinderte, dass nach der schnellen Ankunft der Verwandten aus diesen Verletzungen Knochenbrüche und schwerste Verletzungen wurden.

Ich wurde im Zimmer des Gefängnisdirektors abgeliefert, der mit Freunden das Ende des Fastenmonats feierte. Colonel Barakat war im Zivilleben Französischlehrer und freute sich, dass er den Unfall mit mir auf Französisch besprechen konnte. Er ging mit mir in den Frauentrakt des Gefängnisses, wo ich, wie er erwartet hatte, angesichts der schockierenden Zustände zur Salzsäule erstarrte. Dann folgte der leichte Umbau des Dienstzimmers zur Unterbringung der Gefangenen: eine bequeme Liege, ein Teetischchen (Erinnerung an Izmir), die Übergabe eines sehr großen Schlüssels. Es war der Schlüssel des riesigen Tors zum Bau der Osmanenzeit, der für den Fall, dass ich nachts einmal… da ich ja nicht durch den Frauentrakt zu den Toiletten im Männertrakt gehen konnte… den Weg unter die nahe gelegene Brücke über den Orontes eröffnet hätte.

Ich schlief erschöpft und mit dem gewaltigen Schlüssel auf dem Tischchen neben mir ein und erwachte am nächsten Morgen von dem Stimmengewirr vor

Das erste Projekt: Aufnahmen im Nordsyrischen Kalksteinmassiv

meiner Tür. Ich wurde besucht mit Festtagsgebäck: Der nächtliche Unfall und vor allem die Frage, *„was hatten Sie denn um Himmels willen in Beirut zu tun?"* wurden immer wieder von vorne diskutiert. Ungewöhnlich schnell wurde der Unfall vor Gericht verhandelt, ich wurde zur Zahlung eines nicht zu hohen Geldbetrags an die beiden Fahrer verurteilt und konnte nach Ankunft meiner Architekten mit provisorischer Frontscheibe nach Aleppo fahren. Sollte jetzt der Eindruck entstanden sein, ich würde Unfälle magnetisch anziehen – der Unfall in Hama war nicht der letzte, den ich in Syrien überlebte.

Am 22. September fuhren wir nach El Bara, zu Nacharbeiten nach Ruweiha, Mudjleyya und Frikya sowie zum ersten Mal zu der Moschee im Nachbarort Kafr Ruma (Taf. 3). Unvergesslich ist mir der Empfang beim *Muchtar* des Ortes: Die Frauen – ungewöhnlich groß, schlank, schön – begegneten mir so heiter und unbeschwert, wie ich es in keiner Siedlung vorher erlebt hatte...

In El Bara war unsere Stimmung so trist wie beim letzten Aufenthalt: In der Hauptkirche des 5. Jahrhunderts war der große Türsturz der Westseite gedreht worden und der Dekor der Stirnseite, auf dem sich die antike farbige Fassung außergewöhnlich gut erhalten hatte, war monatelang der Witterung ausgesetzt gewesen[21]. Mein Brief nach Damaskus mit der Bitte, diesen außergewöhnlichen Sturz zum Museum zu transportieren, blieb ohne Erfolg. In der Transeptkirche hatten, nur zu gut sichtbar, Raubgrabungsarbeiten des Antikenwächters begonnen. Ich konnte Abu Aboud nur darauf hinweisen, dass ich im nächsten Jahr wiederkommen würde, erwartete, alle Kapitelle unverändert vorzufinden, und wenn nicht...

Eine große Überraschung waren die wiederverwendeten Kapitelle im Inneren der Moschee von Kafr Ruma: In ihr wiederholte sich der Befund einiger Kapitelle der Transeptkirche und ließ eine Werkstatt des 6. Jahrhunderts erkennen, die entschieden über die Kapitelle von Qalʿat Simʿan hinausführte[22]. Meine Fotos der Reise von 1971 zeigten, dass verwandte Kapitelle sich auch im Hof der Moschee von Maʿarret en Noman befanden und sogar zur Kirche in Qasr ibn Wardan, also zu einem weit entfernten Ort Zentralsyriens führten. Auch das Gesamtbild, das die Weitarkaden-Basilika von Ruweiha durch den Verzicht auf Ornamentik im spartanisch ausgestatteten Innenraum in deutlichen Kontrast zur Basilika von Qalbloze stellte, führte noch einmal zur Reise von 1971, d. h. zur Weitarkadenbasilika von Resafa zurück.

Damit war klar, dass meine nächste Kampagne zu Orten Zentralsyriens, zu Städten im direkten Einflussbereich des Bergmassivs – Hama, Idlib, Maʿarret en Noman – und vor allem zu der einzigen wenigstens teilweise erhaltenen Kirche des 6. Jahrhunderts in Aleppo, dem antiken Beroea führen würde (Taf. 2). Bei meinem Treffen mit dem Direktor des Museums in Aleppo sprach ich die Chance für eventuelle Aufnahmen in der Madrasa al-Hallawiya, der ehemaligen Hauptkirche von Beroea an, und seine Reaktion war positiv. Im Anschluss an meinen Arbeitsbericht an den Generaldirektor in Damaskus stellte ich den Antrag auf Kapitellaufnahmen in der Madrasa al-Hallawiya.

Nach zwei Wochen Arbeit in Qalʿat Simʿan zusammen mit Ulrike Hess fuhr ich mit ihr zusammen zurück nach Beirut, um noch einmal Georges Tchalenko zu treffen. Bei der Einfahrt in Beiruts Viertel Aschrafiye traf mich tief der Anblick der durchlöcherten und zerstörten Häuser. Ich verlor die Orientierung und kam unter ständigem Schimpfen der neben mir sitzenden Architektin irgendwie hinunter zur Uferstraße. Unbeschreiblich die Fahrt durch das Zentrum zum Deutschen Orientinstitut, wo wir mit dem Satz empfangen wurden: *„Es wäre wohl besser gewesen, nicht zu kommen"*. Die Stadt war zweigeteilt in West- und Ostbeirut. Es war mehr als nur leichtsinnig von mir mit dem VW-Bus in den Ostteil zu fahren, um Georges Tchalenko abzuholen, aber... Da saßen wir nun im Orientinstitut und besprachen die Ergebnisse der Kampagne. Georges Tchalenko war froh, die so erfreulich guten Zeichnungen von Ulrike Hess vor Augen zu haben und auch erleichtert, über seine katastrophale Situation sowie die miserable Lage des Bemabuches berichten zu können – alles war gut und zugleich zutiefst deprimierend.

1977. Rückfahrt mit dem Schiff von Beirut aus über Alexandria nach Venedig

Die Rückfahrt nach Europa gestaltete sich schwieriger als erwartet, denn das Schiff der Turkish Maritime Line war von Mekkapilgern gekapert worden. Henri Pharaon fuhr mit uns und seinem Agenten zum Hafen von Beirut und verhandelte. In der Zwischenzeit war Ulrike in eine gefährliche Situation gekommen: Sie schoss ein Foto nach dem anderen von den Leuten, die vor den Kellerlöchern ihrer zerstörten Häuser saßen und war in Sekunden von einer wütenden Menschengruppe eingekesselt. Ohne die Vermittlung des Agenten wäre es schlecht ausgegangen. Dann kam die Lösung unserer Probleme: Henri Pharaon hatte ein dänisches Schiff mit reichlich Bezahlung ‚gepachtet'. Wir wurden mit dem VW-Bus verladen und gemeinsam mit zahllosen Kakerlaken nach Alexandria transportiert. Die Rückfahrt mit einem Schiff der Adriatica nach Venedig war luxuriöser als alle Fahrten, die ich bis dahin erlebt hatte.

1978. Ende der Aufnahmen in Qalʿat Simʿan

1977 hatte ich eine Kopie meiner Habilitationsarbeit und einen gerade erschienenen Artikel über Qalʿat Simʿan zusammen mit den Plänen für die vierte Kampagne an Ernest Will geschickt. 1978 begann ein Briefwechsel, der sich im Jahr 1979 fortsetzte und meine Situation im Kalksteinmassiv grundlegend veränderte. Ich hatte beantragt, detaillierte Aufnahmen zu einzelnen der von mir aufgenommenen Säulenkapitelle in Qalʿat Simʿan machen zu können. Dazu hatte ich um die Genehmigung für die Publikation der zeichnerischen Aufnahmen von circa 12 Türen und Gesimsen gebeten und hatte den Transport der gefährdeten und besonders wichtigen Kapitelle von Bafetin in ein Museum für sinnvoll gehalten. Die Publikation der Kapitelle von Qalʿat Simʿan wurde mir mit dem Hinweis auf unmittelbar bevorstehende Aufnahmen einer französischen *Équipe* untersagt: „*J. P. Sodini et moi-meme avions formé le projet d'une étude plus approfondie consacrée à Qalat Seman ... Cette étude peut commencer des cette année par des relevés consacrés au décor ornamental*" (Brief von Ernest Will vom 26. Februar 1979). Für meine Aufnahme von 12 Türen wurde mir die umfassende Aufnahme aller(!) Türen des Kalksteinmassivs vonseiten des Institut Français in naher Zukunft angekündigt; der Transport von gefährdeten Kapitellen an das Museum in Aleppo wurde untersagt.

Was aber geschah, war folgendes: Die Kapitelle des 5. Jahrhunderts waren in die Konzession für meine Bearbeitung der Kapitelle des 4. bis 6. Jahrhunderts eingeschlossen und wurden von mir 1993 zusammen mit einer kleinen Auswahl von Türen und Gesimsen publiziert (Taf. 16b). Nach den letzten Berichten über die Situation des Baukomplexes nach 2011 war ein großer Teil der Säulenkapitelle schon vor 2016 verschwunden oder beschädigt, die Pfeilerkapitelle dagegen waren weitgehend erhalten geblieben. Von Luftangriffen und Granateinschlägen wurden 2016 vor allem das Oktogon und die Eingangsfassade des Südarmes der kreuzförmigen Anlage getroffen – darauf werde ich später zurückkommen (Taf. 12b).

Der Transport gefährdeter Kapitelle in das Museum von Aleppo durch Georges Tchalenko vor vielen Jahren war sehr sinnvoll gewesen, denn nur dadurch blieb wenigstens ein Kapitell der Kirche von Qasr ibn Wardan gut erhalten. Die Kapitelle von Bafetin, von uns in der vierten Kampagne detailliert aufgenommen, wurden vor 1990 in den Antikenhandel abtransportiert. Sie wurden von mir 2002 publiziert.

1979. Vierte Kampagne: Aufnahmen in der Madrasa al-Hallawiya und in Qasr ibn Wardan

Im Jahr 1979 fanden die ersten Aufnahmen außerhalb des Kalksteinmassivs statt, denn ich hatte die Genehmigung für die Madrasa al-Hallawiya erhalten und war von Kamel Schehade zur Aufnahme der Kapitelle nach Qasr ibn Wardan eingeladen worden.

Da keine einzige der ehemals zahlreichen Kirchen innerhalb der Mauern Antiochias erhalten ist oder freigelegt werden konnte, war die Genehmigung für Aufnahmen in der Madrasa al-Hallawiya ein Göttergeschenk (Taf. 8. 9). In der Kirche neben der Koranschule, die der Überlieferung nach die Hauptkirche des antiken *Beroea*, des heutigen Aleppo war, blieben Säulenstellungen mit ihren Kapitellen erhalten, die von großer Bedeutung für das Verständnis der Baudekoration des Kalksteinmassivs sind (Taf. 9a. b). Kapitellfotos in älterer Literatur ließen Wesentliches nicht erkennen, da alle Elemente übertüncht worden waren[23].

Nun wurden alle Kapitelle des Innenraumes aufgenommen (Taf. 9a. b) und vor allem ihre übertünchten Einzelmotive in Detailskizzen festgehalten[24]. Das Ergebnis war faszinierend, da ich so den Beziehungen der Kapitelle einer nordsyrischen Stadt zu den Befunden im Kalksteinmassiv nachgehen konnte (Taf. 16b. c). Als die Madrasa al-Hallawiya 2014 bei den Kämpfen in der Altstadt von Aleppo durch Granateinschläge und anschließenden Brand schwer beschädigt wurde (Taf. 8b. 9c), traf es besonders schwer die von uns detailliert aufgenommenen Kapitelle des Westteils (Taf. 9a. b). Nicht zum ersten Mal war ich dankbar, dass ich vor der Zerstörung zusammen mit einer Architektin eine detaillierte Aufnahme anfertigen konnte.

Im VW-Bus hatte ich zwei Speziallleitern mitgebracht, die Heike Fastje bei der zeichnerischen Aufnahme einiger Kapitelle unterstützten und mir die detaillierte Aufnahme jedes Kapitells ermöglichten. Das Ergebnis war aufregend: Alle über Qalʿat Simʿan hinausführenden Neuerungen traten als Grundformen auf den Kapitellen auf und führten zu Kapitell- und Türformen des 6. Jahrhunderts (Taf. 16b. c). Einiges sprach dafür, dass diese Neuerungen auch in der Metropole Antiochia bekannt waren, doch musste offenbleiben, in welchem Maß das Bild der Kirche von Beroea auf die Metropole übertragbar war.

Das erste Projekt: Aufnahmen im Nordsyrischen Kalksteinmassiv

Mit dieser neuen Dokumentation fuhren wir zu detaillierten Aufnahmen nach El Bara, Bakirha und Bafetin, sowie zu den Museen von Hama, Idlib, Maʿarret en Noman und Aleppo. In Bafetin wurden wir in der Kirche des 6. Jahrhunderts von dem plötzlichen Kontrollbesuch von Ernest Will und Jean-Pierre Sodini überrascht. Heike Fastje zeichnete gerade eines der Kapitelle und ich schrieb in mein Tagebuch: Was wäre wohl geschehen, wenn ich gerade eine der nicht genehmigten Türen vermessen hätte? Ich stand auf, teilte Heike mit, dass ich für circa eine Stunde zur Kirche von Mshabbak fahren würde, und verschwand.

Bei dem Aufenthalt in Qasr ibn Wardan (Taf. 10) trafen wir auf die schon weit fortgeschrittenen Grabungen und Restaurierungen von Kamel Schehade und brachten als Gastgeschenk die beiden Spezialleitern mit. Wir konnten die bisher bekannten Kapitelle durch die gerade freigelegten ergänzen[25]. Wir übernachteten in einem der wenigen Lehmziegelhäuser, die damals noch nicht zu einem durch zahlreiche Hausbauten erweiterten Dorf gehörten.

Die Asphaltstraße nach Qasr ibn Wardan war 1979 noch nicht fertiggestellt und die Pisten zu weiter im Inneren gelegenen Orten war mit dem Pickup von Kamel Schehade nur einigermaßen zu bewältigen. Dies ist mir besonders in Erinnerung, weil ich damals zum ersten Mal querfeldein nach al-Andarin kam, von dem Kamel Schehade Wunderdinge erzählt hatte. In einer der dortigen Kirchen gebe es noch weitere Kapitelle von der Art in der Kirche von Qasr ibn Wardan, wurde berichtet. Erst kurz vor Sonnenuntergang kamen wir nach einer strapaziösen Fahrt mit dem Pickup zur dortigen Südkirche und im letzten Dämmerlicht nahm ich einige dieser Kapitelle auf – ich ahnte nicht, dass ich achtzehn Jahre später Grabungsarbeiten in eben diesem Ort beginnen würde.

Hin- und Rückfahrt führten in diesem Jahr nicht mehr in den Libanon, sondern in die Türkei: Venedig-Izmir-Venedig: Die Informationen, die wir vom deutschen Orientinstitut in Beirut und von Georges Tchalenko erhielten, sprachen dafür, dass sich die Situation im Libanon gegenüber 1977 noch einmal verschlechtert hatte.

Besonders traurig war die Nachricht, dass Georges Tchalenko die Publikation der zeichnerischen Aufnahmen zu den *„Églises syriennes à bêma"* nicht selbst betreuen durfte. Sie waren 1979 unter dem Titel *„Églises de villages"* und nicht mit Tchalenko als Autor, sondern mit der Angabe *„Dessins établis sous la direction de Georges Tchalenko par Edgar Baccache"* erschienen. Dies war für das Buch eine überaus problematische Entscheidung, Edgar Baccache war an keiner der Aufnahmen im Kalksteinmassiv beteiligt war und hatte jahrelang unter der Leitung von Tchalenko dessen Bleistiftzeichnungen in Tusche umgesetzt. Es war klar, dass mit der Änderung des Titels, der Aufhebung der von Tchalenko vorgesehenen Trennung von Zeichnungen für den Textband auf der einen und Zeichnungen für den Tafelband auf der anderen Seite, sowie der Entscheidung für das vom Autor vehement abgelehnte Großformat eine Publikation ohne Mitsprache des Autors eingeleitet worden war. Als Rechtfertigung wurde in den Briefen von Ernest Will und Georges Tate hervorgehoben, dass Tchalenko nur für den Text und nicht für die Zeichnungen und Fotos ein Autorenrecht besaß.

1980. Nacharbeit im Kalksteinmassiv; Vorbereitung einer Syrien-Ausstellung

Als ich im Frühjahr 1980 zur Vorbereitung der Syrienausstellung „Land des Baal" nach Damaskus kam, hatte sich dort die Situation durch die Gründung der Außenstelle des Deutschen Archäologischen Instituts in Berlin verändert. Es gab nun eine Kontaktstelle für alle in Syrien arbeitenden Archäologen. Auch meine persönliche Situation hatte sich verändert: Ich war auf eine Professur an der Universität Heidelberg berufen worden und würde dort im Sommersemester 1980 die Lehre beginnen.

Zusammen mit dem Team von Eva Strommenger[26] bereitete ich die Auswahl der Objekte im Museum von Damaskus vor und fuhr für diese Ausstellung zum ersten Mal zum Kloster Mar Jakub bei Qara, zum Kloster Mar Aelian 10 km vor Qaryatain und nach Halawe am Euphrat. Die anschließenden Nacharbeiten im Kalksteinmassiv konzentrierten sich auf Kirkbize, Banakfur, Ishruk und Meʿez. Zum letzten Mal konnte ich die Gastfreundschaft im Haus des Antikenwächters Abu Feisal genießen, denn das französische Team hatte für die Arbeiten in Deḥes die Schule von Sermada gemietet.

Ich hatte gehofft, Georges Tchalenko in Damaskus treffen zu können, doch war allein ein Telefonkontakt realisierbar. Die mit dem Druck des Bemabuches verbundenen Ereignisse hatten sich noch einmal verschärft: Nach der Publikation des ersten Bandes erschien 1980 der Band mit den Fotos von Georges Tchalenko unter dem Namen von Edgar Baccache, der kein einziges der Fotos angefertigt hatte, in dem Großformat, das Tchalenko immer abgelehnt hatte. Bei allen Rückfragen wurde noch einmal darauf hingewiesen, dass alle Aufnahmen, die Georges Tchalenko, finanziert vom Institut Français angefertigt hatte, Besitz des Instituts seien, und der Autor allein ein Recht für den Text habe. Georges

Das erste Projekt: Aufnahmen im Nordsyrischen Kalksteinmassiv

Tchalenko hoffte, die Gesamtsituation des Buches in seinem Vorwort zum Textband klären zu können.

Ich kannte den Textband seit 1971 und wollte – trotz aller Mahnungen von Tchalenko, die Publikation meines Buches nicht an sein Buch zu binden – die Publikation seines Textbandes abwarten. Er erschien 1990, erst drei Jahre nach seinem Tod und ohne das Vorwort, für das er mit Unterstützung eines Anwalts gekämpft hatte.

Der erste Band meiner Arbeit in den 70er Jahren erschien 1993, nach der Publikation „aller Türen" von Alice Naccache, der zweite Band 2002, d. h., nach dem Beginn von Grabungsarbeiten in al-Andarin. Die 1979 angekündigte Arbeit von Jean Pierre Sodini zur Baudekoration von Qalʿat Simʿan wird noch erwartet, doch einige Berichte über dortige Arbeiten kamen heraus: Die Bearbeitung des großen Zentrums durch das französische Institut hatte begonnen.

1989–1990. Reise zu den Ruinenorten des Bergmassivs, die jetzt zur Türkei gehören

Während meiner Kampagnen im Kalksteinmassiv war ich auf der Straße zur Grenzstation Bab al-Hawa oft am Kloster Qasr el Banat vorbeigekommen. Nur einmal war ich für wenige Minuten zu ihm hinaufgegangen, denn es liegt im Grenzland zwischen Türkei und Syrien. Anfang 1989 erhielt ich einen Brief von der syrischen Archäologin Widad Khoury, die in den 80er Jahren Arbeiten in den antiken Siedlungen des Djebel Wastani begonnen hatte, einer Region des Kalksteinmassivs, die Georges Tchalenko in sein Buch über die „Villages antiques" nicht eingeschlossen hatte.

Widad Khoury teilte mir mit, dass sie durch Beziehungen nach Antiochia, dem heutigen Antakya eine Genehmigung zum Besuch der Orte im militärischen Sperrgebiet erhalten könnte. Ich war mitten in den Vorbereitungen für den Druck von Band I zur Baudekoration und beschloss sofort, noch einmal nach Syrien zu fliegen. Wir trafen uns in Idlib im Haus von Souad, der Direktorin der dortigen Grundschule und bereiteten den Besuch in El Bara sowie die Reise ins Niemandsland vor.

Ich fuhr zuerst einmal nach Bashmishli, um nach zehn Jahren die Familie von Abu Feisal wiederzusehen. Das Dorf hatte inzwischen einen Wasserturm und im Haus von Abu Feisal gab es sogar einen Fernseher. In dem kleinen Tchalenko-Haus übernachtete jetzt ab und zu ein Tourist, denn Touristen, so erfuhr ich, kamen jetzt viel häufiger als früher. Abu Feisal stellte mir seinen Nachfolger vor und bat mich, ihn nach Bshendlaya zu fahren, wo es den besten Tabak gab (Taf. 3). Ich ging, d. h. fuhr zuerst einmal über die neue Asphaltstraße nach Bakirha und Dar Qita. Vor der Sergiuskirche parkte ein Minibus mit Touristen. Auch ich stellte meinen Leihwagen ab und ging ins Innere der Kirche. In jeder Kirche traf ich auf gestörte Fundlagen, von mir aufgenommene Kapitelle waren beschädigt oder nicht mehr auffindbar. Ich konnte mir unschwer vorstellen, wie leicht es geworden war, Pickups vor den Bauten zu parken und Objekte aufzuladen... Ich stieg auf der Fahrt nach Bshendlaya unterwegs nicht mehr aus, besuchte keinen der von Bashmishli aus erreichbaren antiken Orte. Falsche Sentimentalität? Nein, das war eine Veränderung, die ich nicht besichtigen wollte.

Schon vor unserer Ankunft in El Bara hatten wir am Museum in Idlib erfahren, dass der Sohn von Abu Aboud ein Kapitell in Lattakia hatte verkaufen wollen, dort von der Polizei verhaftet wurde und das Kapitell nach El Bara zurückbringen musste. Nach der Ankunft fragten wir also direkt nach diesem Kapitell. Ich stand vor dem Kapitell mit umlaufenden Arkaden aus der Transeptkirche, von dem ich angenommen hatte, dass es nach meiner Aufnahme in seinem tiefen Loch, abgedeckt durch einen Haufen Quader ‚gesichert' war[27]. Der Sohn von Abu Achmed wurde einige Jahre später als Nachfolger seines Vaters als Antikenwächter eingesetzt.

Ein letzter Schock in El Bara war der Wiederaufbau der kleinen von Jean-Pascal Fourdrin[28] aufgenommenen Kirche durch einen syrischen Architekten. Er hatte es geschafft, nicht nur im Inneren, sondern auch auf der Nordfassade alles falsch einzusetzen. War keiner auf die Idee gekommen, ihm eine der alten Ansichten der Fassade zu kopieren? Mit Widad Khoury fuhr ich noch einmal in die Orte des Djebel Zawiye, in denen ich gearbeitet hatte. Unser Bericht über Elemente von Baudekoration – am Straßenrand aufgestellt, fertig für den Abtransport – wurde an der Generaldirektion in Damaskus mit einigen Kommentaren zu der Reise der beiden Damen aufgenommen.

Ich bin noch heute rundherum dankbar für den so ganz anderen Tag in Qasr el Banat, Herbet Tezin und Kasr Iblisu, den Orten im Grenzland. Widad Khoury hatte die Genehmigung erhalten und wir gingen, begleitet von türkischem Militär, hinauf in die schwer zugänglichen Orte des Djebel Barisha. Der Zauber dieser verlassenen und nicht nachbesiedelten Orte teilte sich jedem von uns mit. In Hochstimmung kamen wir zurück zur türkischen Militärstation und feierten den Abschied vom Grenzland.

2016–2019. Zur Situation in Qalʿat Simʿan nach 2011

Als ich 2014 den ersten Bericht über Vandalismus in der kreuzförmigen, um die Säule Simeons errichteten Anlage erhielt, hatte ich noch keine Vorstellung von dem Ausmaß der Zerstörungen bei allen Bauten auf dem Hochplateau zwischen 2016 und 2019. Die ausführlichen Berichte durch das Team der *Syrians for Heritage Association* – nicht nur über Qalʿat Simʿan, sondern auch über zahlreiche Orte im Kalksteinmassiv – waren für mich mehr als nur schockierend[29].

Es wird berichtet, dass Qalʿat Simʿan schon 2012 nicht mehr durch das „*General Directorate of Antiquities and Museums (DGMA) or any other specialized authority that may be able to maintain the site and enforce its protection*" kontrolliert wurde. 2016 trafen mehrfache Bombadierungen, Granaten- und Raketeneinschläge die Eingangsfassade des südlichen Kreuzarms und das Oktogon des Baukomplexes. Eine explodierende Rakete traf nicht nur die die Säule und ihr Podest, sie beschädigte auch die umgebenden Pfeilerstellungen mit ihren Archivolten. In der Ostkirche wurde darüber hinaus auch noch der Mosaikboden des 10. Jahrhunderts ausgeraubt.

Der Kommentar des Berichtes zu den komplett leeren Innenräumen der Kreuzarme lautet: „*The most alarming activity however, was inside the church where the eastern and northern basilica floors where completely washed away, including the columns bases*"[30] – eine groteske Situation: Nachdem die Säulen der Kreuzarme umgestürzt waren, wurden ihre Kapitelle in den 1940er und 1950er Jahren vor den Innenwänden der Außenmauern, auf den Säulenbasen und teilweise im westlichen Außenbereich aufgestellt. Dort nahm ich sie in den 1970er Jahren auf und publizierte sie 1993. Die Säulen und Kapitelle waren schon vor 2016 größtenteils nicht mehr vorhanden und in einer vollkommen unsinnigen Aktion wurden nun auch noch die Säulenbasen entfernt[31].

Die Apsisdekoration der Ostkirche ist noch nicht zerstört (Taf. 16a) und die Kapitelle der Säulenstellungen wurden 1993 publiziert. Ich blicke mit einem Kapitell der Ostkirche (Taf. 16b) zurück auf die Kapitelle der Madrasa al-Hallawiya (Taf. 9a. b) und die Kapitelle der Kirche von Deir Sambul (Taf. 9c): In Zukunft könnte die Leere des Innenraumes mit einer Dokumentation der alten Aufnahmen gefüllt werden. Der Blick nach Aleppo und in den Süden des Bergmassivs könnte den Kontakt zwischen den auf hohem Niveau arbeitenden lokalen Werkgruppen und den in den großen Städten tätigen Werkgruppen veranschaulichen[32].

Ich hatte 2006 das Ausbuddeln und Abtransportieren der Säulenbasen in der Kirche im Hof des Kastrons von Androna erlebt. Ich wurde damals aufgeklärt, dass Säulenbasen gut verkäuflich, weil bei Neubauten gut verwendbar seien. Nie hätte ich es für möglich gehalten, dass in Qalʿat Simʿan Vergleichbares geschehen könnte. Vielleicht werde ich eines Tages erfahren, warum die Kreuzarme vollständig ausgeräumt wurden…

Ich konnte mir erst nach den Berichten der SIMAT, der ‚Syrians for Heritage Association' einigermaßen vorstellen, wie es möglich war, während der militärischen Auseinandersetzungen in Qalʿat Simʿan auch noch Raubgrabungen durchzuführen: Die Berichte über die Situation in den Ruinenorten des Kalksteinmassivs belegen, dass in den Kriegsjahren jegliche Kontrolle über Steinraub, Antikenraub, Raubgrabung verlorengegangenen war.

2019. Publikation der Restaurierungen von G. Tchalenko in Qalʿat Simʿan durch J. Tchalenko

Nachdem ich den 1990 erschienenen Textband zu den „*Églises Syriennes*" erhalten hatte, blieb ich über 30 Jahre hin in Kontakt mit John Tchalenko, der den Nachlass seines Vaters verwaltete. Ich besprach mit ihm die Publikation des Berichtes über die Restaurierungsarbeiten seines Vaters in Qalʿat Simʿan. Schon 1993 hatte ich auf die so wichtige Publikation der Restaurierungen hingewiesen[33], doch John Tchalenko erwartete die Verhinderung des Drucks von französischer Seite aus und schob die Publikation immer wieder hinaus. Sie erschien nun erst 32 Jahre nach dem Tod seines Vaters mit einer großartigen Biographie und einem Überblick über seine wichtigsten Publikationen.

Die Publikation kam zu einem Zeitpunkt, der daran zweifeln lässt, dass die Restaurierung der Weltkulturerbestätte mit auch nur annähernd so gut ausgebildeten Werkleuten und mit einem vergleichbar hohen Anspruch der Architekten wird stattfinden können.

Ich passe meinen Bericht nicht korrigierend oder erweiternd der vorliegenden Publikation an, weil er auf meinen Gesprächen und dem Briefwechsel mit Tchalenko in den Jahren 1971–1983 beruht und Ereignisse anspricht, die in der Publikation nicht thematisiert wurden. Ich bin John Tchalenko dankbar, in dem Buch nach so vielen Jahren das Vorwort Tchalenkos zu dem Textband der „*Églises Syriennes à bêma*" vorzufinden, für das er jahrelang vergeblich mit seinem Anwalt gekämpft hatte[34]. Ich bin nun nicht mehr die Einzige, für die die letzte

Das erste Projekt: Aufnahmen im Nordsyrischen Kalksteinmassiv

große Publikation von Georges Tchalenko unlösbar mit den Ereignissen in den Jahren 1972–1987 verbunden ist.

Bei meinen Arbeiten im Kalksteinmassiv hatte ich mich so verhalten wie Howard Crosby Butler und seine Mitarbeiter, wenn auch in viel kleinerem Rahmen: Soweit meine Kräfte und meine Ausstattung es zuließen, nahm ich eine bestimmte, im Oberflächenbefund erreichbare Gruppe von Objekten in circa 60 Ruinenorten auf. Es gab allerdings einen großen Unterschied: Das Kalksteinmassiv war französisches Konzessionsgebiet geworden. Die Bewilligung von Konzessionen wird in Zukunft wahrscheinlich anders aussehen. Die Ruinenorte des Nordsyrischen Kalksteinmassivs sind 2011 Unesco-Weltkulturerbe geworden und in Zukunft werden die gewaltigen Probleme der Restaurierung im Vordergrund stehen. Überlegungen zum Umgang mit den Aufnahmen syrischen Kulturgutes, die vor 2011 angefertigt wurden, werde ich nach der Vorstellung meines zweiten Projektes vorstellen.

Das zweite Projekt: Grabungsarbeiten in al-Andarin, dem antiken Androna

Al-Andarin, das antike Androna, ist einer der größten Ruinenorte in der zentralsyrischen Wüstensteppe (Taf. 2. 17). Mit seinen zwei Umfassungsmauern, zehn Kirchen, zwei Badanlagen, einem großen Kastron (*castrum*) und zahlreichen Hausbauten bedeckt er ein Areal von 155 Hektar. Im Jahr 1997 begannen in al-Andarin / Androna Grabungsarbeiten als Zusammenarbeit eines syrischen, eines britischen und eines deutschen Teams.

Drei Jahre nach der Publikation der Grabungsarbeiten des deutschen Teams im Oktober 2015[35] fuhr die Journalistin Karin Leukefeld, begleitet von syrischem Militär, nach al-Andarin / Androna. Sie schickte mir die Fotos der Zerstörung der Grabungsarbeit von neun Kampagnen durch den Islamischen Staat. Die Fotos der Ruine des Grabungshauses und die Trümmerberge der mit Dynamit gesprengten Haupträume des Kastrons hängen nun neben den alten Aufnahmen an der Wand vor meinem Computer.

Im Zentrum der Zerstörung standen das Westtor und die hoch anstehenden Räume der Westseite des Kastrons, die von uns 2004 restauriert worden waren (Taf. 27. 29. 30b). Doch nicht der circa zehn Meter hoch anstehende Rest des Apsisbogens der Hauptkirche, des Wahrzeichens von Androna[36], sondern die bis zur Höhe von sechs Metern erhaltenen Teile des Kastrons wurden gesprengt. Bei ihrem zweiten Aufenthalt in Androna stellte Karin Leukefeld fest, dass die Toranlage an der Südseite des Kastrons nicht zerstört wurden.

Im Frühjahr 2006 war das ‚Fest der Wüste / Steppe' in Androna gefeiert worden. Der Bürgermeister von Hama hatte eine Broschüre für die Festgäste herausgegeben, deren Fotos genau die Teile des Kastrons zeigen, die 2016 zerstört wurden (Taf. 32a. b). Es drängte sich die Überlegung auf, ob es vielleicht einen Zusammenhang zwischen dem Ereignis 2006 und den Aktivitäten 2016 gebe.

1996. Rückkehr nach Syrien; Vorbereitung der Ausgrabung

Als der Generaldirektor der syrischen Antikendirektion Ali Abu Assaf und der ehemalige Leiter des Archäologischen Instituts in Damaskus Michael Meineke in den Jahren nach 1980 anfragten, ob es weiterhin Pläne für eine Grabung in al-Andarin gebe, hatte sich meine persönliche Situation gegenüber den

Als Archäologin in Syrien

70er Jahren grundlegend verändert. In meiner Antwort sprach ich nicht von diesen Veränderungen, sondern verwies darauf, dass die Publikation meiner Arbeit im Kalksteinmassiv noch immer blockiert sei. Trotz bestem Wissen, wie problematisch die Organisation einer Grabung in einem Ruinenort ohne Infrastruktur sein würde, hielt ich die Tür offen und sagte nicht ab. Nach der lang erwarteten Publikation von Band 1 meines ersten Projekts[37] kehrte mein Kopf langsam nach Syrien zurück.

Ich beschloss 1996, zu Vorgesprächen zur Antikendirektion in Damaskus zu fliegen. Bei den Gesprächen in Damaskus wurden nicht nur Grabungsarbeiten in al-Andarin / Androna diskutiert. Inzwischen wesentlich älter, war für mich die Grabungsleitung in einem 155 Hektar großen Ruinenort problematisch. Ich trug zuerst meine Überlegungen zu einem eventuellen Projekt in Qasr ibn Wardan vor: Aufnahme der freigelegten und restaurierten Bauten mit einem Architektenteam und Ausgrabung des dortigen Militärlagers. Leider hielt ein derartiges Projekt der damalige Generaldirektor Sultan Muhesen für nicht sinnvoll, da der Ort bereits Touristenzentrum sei. Die Reaktion auf das geplante Grabungsprojekt in al-Andarin / Androna (hinfort immer Androna), war positiv. Der Grabungsbeginn wurde jedoch von der Organisation einer internationalen Zusammenarbeit abhängig gemacht, an der nach Ansicht des Generaldirektors auf jeden Fall ein französisches Team beteiligt sein sollte.

Die Zusammenarbeit mit einem Team britischer und einem Team syrischer Archäologen konnte ich mir gut vorstellen. Als mir Cyril Mango bei meiner telefonischen Anfrage nach eventuellen Mitarbeitern in Androna mitteilte, dass seine Frau mit einem Team aus Oxford sehr gerne mitarbeiten würde, wurde sofort ein Treffen für den Sommer 1997 organisiert. Danach nahm ich Kontakt zu Abdalrassak Zaqzouq, dem Direktor des Museums in Hama auf. Als er positiv auf meinen Vorschlag für eine Zusammenarbeit reagierte, verschob ich alle Fragen zu der Beteiligung eines französischen Teams auf den Beginn der Grabungsarbeiten.

Nach den Gesprächen in Damaskus stellte ich einen Antrag für die Grabung in Androna bei der Thyssenstiftung, und er wurde für drei Jahre bewilligt. Als Grabungsarchitektin gewann ich Ulrike Hess, die schon im Kalksteinmassiv mitgearbeitet hatte. Die geodätische Aufnahme des Ortes übernahm ein Team der TU Karlsruhe, die Bearbeitung der Kleinfunde sollte in den Händen von Peter Knötzele und Marion Seibel liegen, und als enge Mitarbeiter bei den Grabungsschnitten wurden Ina Eichner und der Grabungstechniker Holger Hirth gewonnen. Der wichtigste Mitarbeiter bei der Organisation der Arbeiten vor

Das zweite Projekt: Grabungsarbeiten in al-Andarin, dem antiken Androna

Grabungsbeginn war Ghassan al Shamat aus Damaskus, den ich am dortigen Deutschen Archäologischen Institut kennengelernt hatte. Folgende Probleme mussten vor Grabungsbeginn gelöst werden:

- Die Unterbringung des Grabungsteams in einem nicht zu weit von Androna entfernten Haus.
- Die tägliche Versorgung des Teams mit Trinkwasser und Lebensmitteln.
- Die Bohrung nach Grundwasser, das – sollte es auch salzhaltig sein – für die Toiletten, die Küchenarbeiten etc. notwendig war.
- Das Anwerben von Arbeitern in den Dörfern der Region und – im Idealfall – auch die Einstellung einer Köchin.

Alle Überlegungen waren eng mit der grundlegend problematischen geographischen Lage des Ruinenortes verbunden (Taf. 17). Er war wie alle Orte Innersyriens von Damaskus wie auch von Aleppo und Hama aus schwer zu verwalten: Die Asphaltstraße nach Aleppo war in miserablem Zustand und die Asphaltstraße zu den größten Nachbarorten von Androna – Homeh und Masluchiyye – war erst wenige Jahre vor Beginn unseres Projektes fertiggestellt worden. Die Region zwischen al-Hamra und Masluchiyye war verwaltungsmäßig offiziell der Administration von Aleppo unterstellt. Doch schon nach den ersten Kampagnen in Androna gingen alle Entscheidungen für den Kommissar als offiziellen Regierungsvertreter sowie die Einstellung und Bezahlung der Wächter am Ruinenort von Damaskus aus – allerdings in Rücksprache mit dem Direktor des Museums und dem Bürgermeister von Hama.

Schnell stellte sich heraus, dass vor Beginn der ersten Kampagne nur ein Teil der Probleme gelöst werden konnte. So wurde beschlossen, mit einem kleinen Team die geodätische Aufnahme des Ortes und die Dokumentation aller an der Oberfläche greifbaren Befunde zu beginnen.

Der damalige Antikenwächter von Androna, Abu Mamduch, hatte sein Haus zur Miete angeboten, da seine Familie in Zelten lebte. Das Haus war ruinös: Berge von leeren Arrakflaschen, kaputte Fenster und Türen, defekte Stromleitungen, verdreckte Wände, die elektrische Pumpe des Brunnens seit Jahren verschwunden und keine irgendwie geartete Toilette. Also fuhr ich mit Ghassan nach Hama zum Einkaufen der Baumaterialien für das Haus und das geplante

Toilettenhäuschen, den Kauf einer elektrischen Pumpe sowie großer Vorräte an Trinkwasser, Bier und allem Lebensnotwendigen.

Mein erster Besuch vor Grabungsbeginn führte zu dem Baukomplex von Qasr ibn Wardan, wo ich seit 1979 nicht mehr gewesen war (Taf. 10). Ich hatte bei der Fahrt nach Hama schon dankbar festgestellt, dass die Asphaltstraße fertig war und nun über den Nachbarort von Androna hinaus bis nach Masluchiye führte. Die von dieser Straße kurz nach dem Ort Homeh abbiegende Piste nach Androna war so schwer befahrbar, dass die Anschaffung eines Geländewagens auf die Liste des absolut Notwendigen kam.

Nachdem Ghassan die Arbeitsgruppe für die Restaurierung des Hauses in Homeh und den Bau des Toilettenhauses organisiert hatte, fuhr ich zurück nach Damaskus. Ich stellte in der Antikenkommission die Mitarbeiter des deutschen Teams und den Plan der geplanten Arbeiten in Androna vor und flog mit dem Vorvertrag für ein internationales-Team nach Deutschland zurück.

1997. Reise nach Syrien im Frühjahr. Im Sommer Survey und geodätische Vermessung

Mir war von Anfang an nur zu sehr bewusst, dass die Betreuung meines Sohnes während der Grabungsmonate eine jedes Jahr neu zu lösende Aufgabe sein würde. Ich reiste darum mit Julian im Frühjahr 1997 nach Syrien, um ihm den Ort zu zeigen, an dem ich mich in den kommenden Jahren für jeweils einige Monate aufhalten würde. Die Reise führte nach einigen Tagen Aufenthalt in Damaskus zuerst nach Qasr ibn Wardan und dann nach Androna. Bei dem anschließenden Aufenthalt in Qal'at Siman wurde uns klar, dass die Reise zu einem späteren Zeitpunkt wiederholt werden sollte. Geplant war sie für die Jahre nach Abschluss der Grabungsarbeiten...

Am 14. August fuhr ich mit dem Range Rover nach Venedig und nach der Ankunft in Izmir mit der türkischen Schifffahrtslinie dann über Konya zur syrischen Grenzstation Bab al-Hawa. Vor Beginn der Arbeiten in Androna musste ich den Arbeitsplan für 1997 an der Antikenkommission in Damaskus vorstellen und die Formulare für die Zusammenarbeit des deutschen mit dem englischen Team ausfüllen. Der Generaldirektor Sultan Muhesen versprach, einen Kommissar nach Home zu schicken und die Mitarbeit eines syrischen Teams aus Hama zu unterstützen – die Frage nach der Beteiligung eines französischen Teams blieb vorläufig offen.

Das zweite Projekt: Grabungsarbeiten in al-Andarin, dem antiken Androna

Mit Ghassan fuhr ich zuerst zu Vorgesprächen mit Abdalrassak Zaqzouq nach Hama und dann weiter nach Qasr ibn Wardan, um mit Abu Hussein (Scheich Ali al Scharif) die Frage der Mitarbeit lokaler Arbeiter zu besprechen.

Die erste Kampagne in Androna im Sommer und Herbst 1997 war ganz der geodätischen Aufnahme und dem Studium der Oberflächenbefunde des riesigen Ortes gewidmet. Nachdem ich mit Ghassan die beiden Geodäten und die Architektin am Flughafen Aleppo abgeholt hatte, wurde im Hotel Ramsis der Beginn der Kampagne gefeiert. Danach ging es zuerst einmal zum Einkaufen in den Souk: Der Range Rover wurde vollgeladen mit Matratzen, Bettwäsche, Töpfen, Geschirr und großen Vorräten an Tee, Kaffee, Reis und Trinkwasser. Da Ghassan zum Glück mit seinem eigenen Auto gekommen war, konnten wir danach alle zusammen nach Homeh fahren.

Unser kleines Team mit dem inzwischen eingetroffenen syrischen Kommissar Nissar Eleki wurde ab 18. September für einige Wochen durch Marlia Mundell Mango, die zukünftige Leiterin des britischen Teams, erweitert, die von ihrem Mann Cyril Mango begleitet wurde. Obwohl der tägliche Ablauf etwas kompliziert war, da Ghassan nach Damaskus zurückgefahren war und wir die Fahrt nach und den Aufenthalt in Androna mit nur einem Auto organisieren mussten, war die Stimmung im September gut.

Die Arbeit der Geodäten begleitete das detaillierte Tagebuch von Ulrike Hess mit der wertvollen Dokumentation der Vermessungsarbeit und ihrer umfangreichen Aufnahme von Einzelobjekten. Ich erkundete Kilometer für Kilometer das 155 Hektar große Gelände und nahm Tag für Tag bis zur Erschöpfung die an der Oberfläche greifbaren Befunde auf. Es dauerte einige Tage, bis ich begriff, dass die zahlreichen runden Trümmerhügel, die wir in den zentralen Regionen von Androna antrafen, zu ehemaligen *Trulli* (Bienenkorbhäusern) gehörten, also Reste der Nachbesiedlung des Ortes waren. Als ich auf den Wegen im Nordteil des Ortes auf eine noch nicht bekannte Kirche und jeden Tag auf die hoch anstehenden Züge der Außenmauer stieß, die in der Publikation von Howard Crosby Butler nicht existiert[38], wurde mir klar, dass alle bisherigen Publikationen nur einen kleinen Teil der großen Siedlung erfasst hatten (Taf. 18).

Wir hatten im August 1997 das renovierte Haus des ehemaligen Antikenwächters bezogen. Zum Glück waren der Bau des Toilettenhäuschens und der Brunnen mit elektrischer Wasserpumpe vor August fertiggestellt, doch die tägliche

Verpflegung und alles für die Arbeiten in Androna Notwendige mussten mit täglichen Fahrten nach Hama und Aleppo organisiert werden.

Wir nahmen mit Einladungen und Gastgeschenken Kontakt zu den fünf Beduinenfamilien des Ortes auf und informierten, dass wir eine Köchin und zwei Arbeiter zur Unterstützung der Arbeit in Androna suchen. Eine Köchin fand sich nach einem Monat im Nachbarort Masluchiye, doch in Homeh war keiner bereit, gegen Bezahlung die Arbeit in Androna zu unterstützen. Kurzum: Es waren wohl diese Situation und die strapaziöse Arbeit im Ruinenort, die zu erheblichen Spannungen zwischen den beiden Geodäten und der Architektin führten. Zwei junge Geodäten und eine erfahrene, fast doppelt so alte Architektin in einer schwierigen, an einem Ort ohne Infrastruktur äußerst strapaziösen Situation. Erst nach der Erkrankung von Ulrike Hess und ihrem Abschied von Androna im Jahr 2004 teilte mir Karsten Malige mit, dass der Bruch zwischen ihm und der Architektin so tiefgehend war, dass alle Arbeiten am Gesamtplan der Siedlung seit 1997 nur noch über Kontaktpersonen abgesprochen wurden. Zu erweiternden Aufnahmen am Stadtplan kehrte Karsten Malige erst 2004 nach Androna zurück.

Der Nachbarort Sammakiya und die Familie Sammakiya

Bei meinen kilometerlangen Wanderungen durch den Ruinenort begegnete ich Mitte August 1997 einem Angehörigen der Familie Sammakiya, der mir nicht nur eine Kopie des Planes mit den ausgedehnten Ländereien rund um Androna gab, sondern auch mit wichtigen Informationen zu diesem ehemaligen Besitz der Familie die Geschichte des Ortes in der ersten Hälfte des 20. Jahrhunderts ansprach.

Bei der Nachbesiedlung des Ruinenortes nach circa 1930 wurden vor allem im Zentrum zahlreiche Bienenkorbhäuser errichtet und dies unter intensiver Verwendung von Elementen der antiken Bauten. In den späten 60er Jahren wurde Androna Staatsgebiet, und alle sekundären Einbauten wurden – trotz der Proteste in umliegenden Dörfern – abgerissen. Zahlreiche Beduinenstämme erkannten in der Folgezeit nicht an, dass Androna nicht mehr privat genutzt werden durfte, und wir hatten die ganze Grabungszeit hindurch Probleme mit der ‚Nutzung' des Ruinenortes.

Ein großer Teil der umfangreichen Ländereien der Familie Sammakiya konnte nach den Landreformen nicht mehr genutzt werden und einige Mitglieder der Familie wanderten aus nach Kanada. Das Haus der Familie in Sammakiya, dem

Nachbarort von Androna, blieb ungenutzt stehen, und ein Wächter betreute den Wohnkomplex mit dem einzigen Baum, den wir 1997 in der Umgebung von Androna antrafen.

Ich ahnte damals nicht, dass die Rückkehr der nach Kanada gegangenen Familie im Jahr 2002 und die folgende Rekultivierung ihrer Ländereien durch Adnan Sammakiya auch die Situation von Androna tiefgreifend verändern würde.

Anwerbung lokaler Arbeiter und Neueinstellung von Antikenwächtern

Als ich Abu Hussein, dem Scheich von Qasr ibn Wardan, von den Problemen bei der Suche nach lokalen Arbeitskräften berichtete, riet er, in der rund 40 Kilometer von Homeh entfernten Siedlung Djenad Arbeiter anzuwerben. Sie seien besser als die Männer aus den Dörfern rund um Androna – ein kostbarer Rat. In den kommenden Jahren waren diese, jeden Tag mit dem großen Pickup von Djenad nach Androna transportierten Arbeiter außerordentlich wichtig für das Gelingen der Grabungsarbeiten im Kastron. Ohne diese erfahrenen Männer hätten wir die Freilegung der 5–6 Meter hohen Grabungsschichten mit tausenden von Basaltquadern und gebrannten Ziegeln nicht bewältigt.

Abu Hussein hatte also nicht Männer aus seinem Dorf oder aus Nachbarorten von Qasr ibn Wardan empfohlen. Ich konnte nach seinen wenigen Informationen rekonstruieren, dass er aufgrund der guten Erfahrungen, die Kamel Schehade mit diesen Arbeitern bei der Freilegung und Rekonstruktion der Bauten von Qasr ibn Wardan gemacht hatte, vorschlug, die Männer aus Djenad als Grabungsarbeiter einzustellen (Taf. 38a).

Die Atmosphäre in Homeh war problematisch: Zwei der fünf Brüder, die mit ihren Familien den Ort beherrschten, hatten sich dem Arrak ergeben. Ein dritter bemühte sich, Mieter für sein gerade fertiggestelltes Haus zu finden. Marlia mietete sich für das kommende Jahr in seinem Haus ein und bat Ghassan, der im September noch einmal für einige Tage nach Androna gekommen war, auch für sie ein Toilettenhäuschen zu bauen.

Der vierte Bruder, in dessen Haus wir wohnten, war offiziell der Antikenwächter von Androna. Wie er diese Aufgabe verstand, erfuhren wir, als wir vom Einkaufen in Hama zurückkamen: Er hatte unsere Abwesenheit genutzt, um antike Objekte zu sichern, die er im Laufe seiner Wächtertätigkeit geraubt und neben einem Pfeiler im Hof des Kastrons vergraben hatte. Er wurde erwischt, kam ins Gefängnis und hoffte, wir würden ihn freikaufen. Hilfe kam von

Als Archäologin in Syrien

Abu Hussein, dem Scheich von Qasr ibn Wardan, dessen Einfluss in der Region groß genug war, um die Freilassung auch ohne Geld durchzusetzen (Taf. 10b).

Schon in den ersten Tagen des Surveys zu den Oberflächenbefunden musste ich feststellen, dass sich der Befund bei Hauptbauten gegenüber meinem ersten Aufenthalt 1979 tiefgreifend verändert hatte: Fassungslos stand ich vor dem tiefen Raubgrabungsloch im Zentrum der Hauptkirche; in der Südkirche war das Mittelschiff ausgeräumt, die Kapitelle, die ich 1979 aufgenommen hatte, waren verschwunden; in der Erzengelkirche hatte der Riss eines Drahtseils den Raub eines Türsturzes verhindert. Zahlreiche Raubgrabungslöcher im Kastron vervollständigten das Bild. Ich hatte begriffen, dass uns das Problem von Raubgrabungen auch in Androna von Anfang an begleiten würde.

In Hama hatte ich die Einstellung von nicht nur einem, sondern von drei Antikenwächtern zu verhandeln, das heißt, jedes Grabungsteam hatte die Bezahlung und Verantwortung für jeweils einen Wächter zu übernehmen.

Wie war die Situation am Ende der ersten Kampagne? Die Vermessung der Siedlung war in den Grundzügen abgeschlossen und die Hauptbauten waren mit den an der Oberfläche greifbaren Informationen erfasst worden. Es blieb jedoch offen, wann die geodätischen Vermessungsarbeiten fortgesetzt werden konnten: Der Gesamtplan von Androna war zu ergänzen durch die zahlreichen Hügel, unter denen vor allem Hausbauten vermutet wurden. So waren es schwerpunktmäßig die Luftaufnahmen, mit denen ich in den folgenden Jahren bei Vorträgen eine direkte Vorstellung von der dichten Besiedlung des 155 Hektar großen Ortes vermitteln konnte (Taf. 19).

Die Einkäufe in Hamra, dem größten Ort der Region (Taf. 17), hatten wir in Hama durch das Angebot im Supermarkt und in den Getränkeläden der Armenier ergänzt. In Sroudj hatte Ghassan den Kontakt zu Chalid al Taki mit seinem großen Pickup hergestellt und so für das kommende Jahr das Problem des täglichen Transports der Arbeiter gelöst. Die Erfahrungen der ersten Monate hatten mir gezeigt, dass ich in Zukunft rund zwei Wochen vor der Ankunft des Grabungsteams zur Vorbereitung der Kampagne in Syrien sein sollte: Ich würde in Qasr ibn Wardan oder Sroudj wohnen und zusammen mit Chalid und Ghassan große Mengen an Trinkwasser und Bier, ausreichend Kaffee, Zucker und Tee, sowie Käse und Marmeladen aus Hama nach Androna transportieren.

Am Ende der ersten Kampagne fuhr ich am 30. September zusammen mit Marlia und Cyril Mango nach Damaskus, brachte meinen Arbeitsbericht zur Antikenkommission und fuhr dann von Bab al-Hawa aus über Konya nach Iz-

Das zweite Projekt: Grabungsarbeiten in al-Andarin, dem antiken Androna

mir. Vor der Schifffahrt nach Venedig rief ich so oft wie möglich Julian an und war kreuzunglücklich, dass ich erst am 12. Oktober wieder zurück sein würde – zu viele Tage nach seinem Geburtstag am 5. Oktober. In allen späteren Kampagnen konnte ich die Grabungsarbeiten so organisieren, dass ich am 5. Oktober zurück in Heidelberg war.

1998. Erste Grabungskampagne; Bohrung nach Grundwasser

Der Anfang der ersten Grabungskampagne war anders organisiert als 1997: Den Schiffstransport des Autos – diesmal war es ein Landrover –, übernahmen zwei Mitarbeiterinnen der Grabung. Ich konnte am 12. August nach Damaskus fliegen, in der Antikenkommission den Arbeitsvertrag für die Grabung unterschreiben und anschließend mit Ghassan über Hama und Qasr ibn Wardan nach Homeh fahren. Bei der Ankunft im gemieteten Haus dann eine böse Überraschung: Die teure elektrische Pumpe war vom Antikenwächter ausgebaut und verkauft worden. Der miserable Zustand des von uns restaurierten Hauses verwies auf das Zelt der Wächterfamilie, das direkt neben dem Haus aufgebaut war.

Als ich mit Ghassan zum Kauf einer neuen Pumpe und zu Einkäufen im Supermarkt in Hama war, berichtete ich Abdalrassak Zaqzouq, dem künftigen Leiter der syrischen Gruppe in Androna, in welchem Zustand wir das Wächterhaus angetroffen hatten und erntete ein breites Grinsen. Nach nur wenigen Minuten im Museumshof bei einem guten Kaffee, ging ich zurück in sein Büro und erkundigte mich, welche Vorschriften beim Bau eines Grabungshauses zu beachten seien.

Es war mir klar, dass wir 1998 noch in Homeh bleiben und von dort aus die Bauarbeiten organisieren mussten. Schon auf unserem Rückweg über Qasr ibn Wardan und Sroudj begannen die Vorgespräche und Vorarbeiten für den Hausbau: Abu Hussein gab die Adresse des Mannes, der nach Wasser bohren würde, ein Onkel von Chalid bot an, mit seiner Arbeitsgruppe den Bau des Hauses zu leiten und in Qasr ibn Wardan würde Abu Hussein den Schmied für Türen und Fenster kontaktieren. Blieb noch die Entscheidung für den Platz, an dem ohne Probleme ein Haus errichtet werden konnte, sowie die Anfertigung der Baupläne durch Ulrike Hess und die Organisation der nötigen Gelder. Als wir mit Ghassan auf der Terrasse des Wächterhauses bei einigen Flaschen Almaza, einem erfrischenden Bier, den schnellen Entschluss feierten, war alles noch unwirklich. Zuerst einmal mussten wir zurück in die Gegenwart und die Ankunft des Grabungsteams vorbereiten.

Vor dem Beginn der Grabungsarbeiten wurde mit dem eingetroffenen Spezialisten nach Wasser gebohrt. Erst in circa 70 Meter Tiefe war das Wasser klar und nicht mehr extrem salzhaltig (Taf. 20a). Von Anfang an war es eine Kostbarkeit: Natürlich war es kein Trinkwasser, doch es bot kurze Erfrischung nach staubiger Arbeit und es ermöglichte den Beginn der Bauarbeiten vor dem Beginn der Grabungsarbeiten.

Bau des Grabungshauses

Ulrike Hess hatte die Pläne für das Grabungshaus gezeichnet und auf ihrer Grundlage wurde parallel zu den Grabungsarbeiten der Baubetrieb organisiert (Taf. 20c. 21). Da Chalid aus Sroudj im Regierungsauftrag mit der Lieferung von Zement und der Produktion von Zementbausteinen betraut war, stand fest, dass das Haus mit Zementbausteinen zu errichten war (Taf. 20c). Wir hatten unseren Traum von der Errichtung mehrerer Bienenkorbhäuser aus Lehmziegeln früh begraben, da er von Anfang an auf Ablehnung stieß.

Unerwartet schwer war der für alle Arbeiten am Ort dringend erforderliche Kauf eines Generators. Es war uns geraten worden, auf keinen Fall ein Produkt aus China zu kaufen, und nach langem Suchen fanden wir einen aus Deutschland nach Aleppo importierten 5000 Watt starken Generator. Ende September war der Rohbau der beiden Toiletten- und der Duschräume, des Arbeitszimmers und der Küche fertiggestellt (Taf. 20c). In großen Wasserbehältern wurde auf dem Dach das Wasser für die Duschen und den Küchenbetrieb gespeichert und erwärmt. Dank einer Spende der Kanzlerin der Universität Heidelberg konnten die ersten Bauarbeiten ohne Probleme bezahlt werden. Alle Folgearbeiten – die Wohnräume mit ihren Eisentüren und Metallgittern für die Fenster, die große Terrasse mit Überdeckung (Taf. 21a) sowie die Einrichtung der Lagerräume – habe ich dann über vier Jahre hin, trotz aller Absagen meiner Anträge auf Unterstützung, irgendwie bewältigt (Taf. 21b).

Das englische Team hatte für alle Kampagnen ein Haus in Homeh gemietet und wollte sich nicht mit der Errichtung eigener Wohnräume am Bau des Hauses beteiligen. Es übernahm aber die Kosten von zwei Räumen des Grabungshauses für die Lagerung ihrer Arbeitsgeräte und Grabungsfunde.

Das zweite Projekt: Grabungsarbeiten in al-Andarin, dem antiken Androna

Schon in der ersten Grabungskampagne hatten wir das Glück, mit Umm Saleh aus dem zwei Kilometer entfernten Sammakiya eine Köchin anzuwerben, die in allen folgenden Kampagnen die gute Seele unseres Teams war (Taf. 39a). In den Nachbarorten konnten die wichtigsten Lebensmittel täglich eingekauft werden; Kartoffeln, Reis, Tomaten, Paprika, Eier, Oliven, Knoblauch und Zwiebeln. Die Kartons mit Bier und Trinkwasser sowie Butter, Milch, verschiedene Sorten Käse und Marmeladen hingegen wurden einmal pro Woche in Hama eingekauft und das leicht Verderbliche in den aus Deutschland mitgebrachten Kühlboxen gelagert.

Die Köchin, die uns 1997 bei der schwierigen ersten Kampagne unterstützt hatte, hatte auf Druck der Familie des ehemaligen Antikenwächters als ehemalige abhängige Landarbeiterin das verdiente Geld bei ihnen abliefern müssen. Der Sohn des Wächters – gerade von mir als Grabungsarbeiter eingestellt – erzählte mit stolz geschwellter Brust, er habe in Hama mit dem Geld eine ganze Nacht eine Tänzerin bezahlt. Dass ihm sofort und für alle Kampagnen das Betreten des Grabungsortes verboten wurde, war nur der Anfang einer Entwicklung, die nach der 1963–1966 eingeführten Landreform einsetzte: Die Spannungen zwischen den einzelnen Dörfern – es gab keine gemeinsamen Gruppen beim Frühstücken und beim Arbeiten – prägten jede Grabungskampagne.

Das Verhältnis zwischen den großen Beduinenfamilien und den ehemals abhängigen Kleinpächtern spielte eine wichtige Rolle bei der Organisation der Grabungsarbeiter. Besonders ausgeprägt waren die Spannungen zwischen den Männern aus Djenad, die bei der Freilegung des Kastrons eingesetzt wurden, und den Mitgliedern der Beduinenfamilien aus Sammakiya und Homeh, die für das deutsche Team bei der Freilegung des großen Hauskomplexes und bei Arbeiten im Bereich der Außenmauer tätig waren. Im britischen und im syrischen Team traf eine Gruppe aus Sammakiya mit Arbeitern aus Qasr ibn Wardan, Sroudj und Tufaha zusammen (Taf. 40a).

Aus dieser von Konflikten geprägten Situation ragt als Positivum die Erfahrung mit den Grabungsarbeitern aus Djenad heraus: In den Landreformen der Baath-Partei (1963–1966 und 1966–1970)[39] hatten sie ein Stück Land erhalten. Als arme, aber selbständige Kleinbauern waren sie in den Grabungsschichten des Kastrons so erfahren im Umgang mit Basaltsteinen und Erdschichten, dass sich ohne Übertreibung sagen lässt: Sie waren die wichtigsten Mitarbeiter der Grabungen im Kastron.

Als Archäologin in Syrien

Schon vor Beginn der Grabungsarbeiten traf ich in Homeh auf eine Situation, die ich nicht erwartet hatte: Anfang September kamen große schwarze Limousinen aus Saudiarabien mit Kühlschränken, Stereoanlagen etc., die bei den Beduinenfamilien abgeliefert und tagelang von Haus zu Haus vorgeführt wurden. Wir erfuhren, dass jede Beduinenfamilie nicht nur mit ‚Luxusgütern', sondern auch in jedem Jahr mit mehreren tausend Dollar unterstützt wurde. Ich konnte mir keinen größeren Gegensatz vorstellen als den zwischen den Dörfern im Nordsyrischen Kalksteinmassiv und den Dörfern der Region von Androna.

1998. Erste Aktivitäten der drei Grabungsteams

Die Schwerpunkte der drei Grabungsteams habe ich in der Grabungspublikation vorgestellt und gehe hier nur kurz auf die Projekte der ersten Kampagnen ein: Das britische Team legte die Badanlage des 6. Jahrhunderts frei (Taf. 23a) und begann mit der Untersuchung der Zisterne vor der Südseite von Androna die Vorarbeiten für die ausgedehnten Untersuchungen zum Wassersystem der ganzen Region[40].

Das syrische Team legte den seiner Funktion nach rätselhaften Bau westlich des Bades frei (Taf. 23b). Schon nach der ersten Kampagne war klar, dass es sich um eine zweite Badanlage handelte, und dieses Ergebnis führte nach dem Fund einer Inschrift zur frűharabischen Zeit in Androna[41]. Die Arbeiten wurden von Abdalrassak Zaqzouq, dem Leiter des Museums von Hama, begonnen und 2000 von seinem Nachfolger Radi Ukhdeh fortgesetzt.

Das deutsche Team begann mit der Freilegung einzelner Trakte des Kastrons (Taf.26), der gewaltigen Anlage im Zentrum von Androna[42]. Die Räume des Kastrons waren auf allen Seiten von einer Erdschicht bedeckt; allein auf der Westseite war der Sturz des Westtors über die Jahrhunderte hin sichtbar geblieben (Taf. 22a).

2000. Erweiterung der Aktivitäten der drei Grabungsteams

Nach dem Ablauf der finanziellen Förderung durch die Thyssenstiftung reichte ich einen Antrag auf Förderung der Grabungsarbeiten für sechs weitere Jahre bei der Deutschen Forschungsgemeinschaft ein. Nach der Bewilligung im Jahr 2000 wurden die Aktivitäten der Grabung erweitert: Die Ausgrabung eines Hauskomplexes im Nordteil und von zwei Toranlagen der Außenmauer – die eine im Nord-, die andere im Südteil des Ortes – wurden vorbereitet (Taf. 18).

Das zweite Projekt: Grabungsarbeiten in al-Andarin, dem antiken Androna

Die offiziellen Kommissare der ersten Kampagnen waren Nissar Eleki, Whafa Zaqqour und Waʿal al Haffian (Taf. 38b). Vor der Erweiterung der Aktivitäten hatte ich gemeinsam mit Marlia Mango bei Bernard Bavant angefragt, ob er als Leiter eines französischen Teams an einer Mitarbeit in Androna interessiert sei – leider war er an seine Arbeit im Kalksteinmassiv gebunden.

Zur gleichen Zeit änderte sich auch das Arbeitsprogramm des britischen Teams: Nach der Ausgrabung der Badanlage und der Untersuchung der Zisterne vor der Südseite von Androna begann der umfangreiche Survey in zahlreichen Orten der Region.

Das syrische Team schloss 2001 die Arbeiten an der früharabisch / omayyadischen Badanlage ab und begann die Ausgrabung eines auf das Jahr 582 n. Chr. datierten Hauses[43].

Die Arbeitssituation der drei Teams war extrem unterschiedlich. Der fast vollständig abgetragenen, nur noch etwas über einen Meter anstehenden frühbyzantinischen (Taf. 23a) wie auch der niedrig erhaltenen früharabisch / omayyadischen Badanlage (Taf. 23b) standen die bis zu 6m hoch anstehenden Räume des doppelgeschossigen Kastrons gegenüber (Taf. 31a. b). Später zeigte sich, dass auch die Räume des Hauskomplexes höher anstanden als die beiden Badanlagen (Taf. 24. 25).

Diese Gegensätze führten dazu, dass allein für die freigelegten Räume des Kastrons und des Hauskomplexes im Jahr 2004 aus Damaskus die Auflagen zur Restaurierung kamen – darauf komme ich später zurück.

Im Vorangehenden wurden die Spannungen zwischen den lokalen Arbeitern aus den Androna benachbarten Dörfern angesprochen. In allen Grabungskampagnen wurden diese Probleme zumindest auf die Mitglieder des deutschen Grabungsteams nicht übertragen. Die Kontakte zu den lokalen Arbeitern und ihren Familien waren nicht nur gut, sie waren die Voraussetzung für den Erfolg der einzelnen Kampagnen. Ich betone dies, weil ich in Androna lernte, den früh einsetzenden Antikenraub durch einzelne lokale Arbeiter von der Gesamterfahrung mit allen lokalen Mitarbeitern zu trennen.

Als Archäologin in Syrien

Mitarbeiter des deutschen Grabungsteams; Kontakte zwischen den drei Grabungsteams

Mit der Erweiterung der Aktivitäten des deutschen Teams nach den ersten drei Grabungskampagnen änderte sich die Zusammensetzung der Mitarbeiter. Die ersten Kampagnen der Grabungsarbeiten im Kastron wurden von Holger Hirth und Ina Eichner geleitet (Taf. 38b). Ulrike Hess (Taf. 41a) arbeitete eng mit ihnen zusammen und fertigte – in Ergänzung ihrer Aufnahmen von 1997 – den Gesamtplan des Kastrons an (Taf. 26). Die Bearbeitung der Keramik und der Kleinfunde lag bis 2001 in den Händen von Peter Knötzele und Marion Seibel (Taf. 38b) und wurde 2003 von Güler Ateş übernommen (Taf. 40).

Die Leitung der Hausgrabung durch Ina Eichner ging nach 2004 auf Fedor Schlimbach über (Taf. 42). In diesen Jahren der Ausweitung der Grabungsarbeiten auf weit auseinanderliegende Bereiche von Androna übernahm Christian Ewert die Aufnahme der Sondagen zum inneren Mauerring, der Basaltmauer (Taf. 40b). Die Aufnahmen der Toranlagen des äußeren Mauerrings (Taf. 26) fanden unter wechselnder Leitung zwischen 2003 und 2006 statt[44].

Als 2004 die Restaurierungsarbeiten begannen, kehrte Karsten Malige nach Androna zurück und begann die Ergänzung des Gesamtplans (Taf. 39b). Die letzte Erweiterung der Aktivitäten begann 2005 mit der Freilegung der Kirche im Hof des Kastrons und ihrer Vermessung und zeichnerischen Aufnahme durch Oliver Hofmeister (Taf. 41b)[45].

Die Kontakte mit dem syrischen Team waren am Anfang leicht zu organisieren, weil ich Abdalrassak Zaqzouq schon aus den Jahren meines ersten Projektes kannte. In den Kampagnen nach der Freilegung der Badanlage wäre das gemeinsame Wohnen am Grabungsort eine Verbesserung gewesen. Doch konnte ein zweites Grabungshaus nicht realisiert werden. Dreimal kamen offizielle Vertreter nach Androna, um eine Stromleitung von Homeh zum Grabungsort zu besprechen – ohne Erfolg. Bei einem eventuellen Neuanfang in Androna wären die mit dem Hausbau verbundenen Grundprobleme zu lösen.

Nach der Ausweitung der Aktivitäten wurde der Austausch zwischen dem deutschen und dem britischen Team erheblich eingeschränkt. In Androna war die Grabung auf drei – bedingt durch die Größe des Ruinenortes – weit auseinanderliegende Baukomplexe aufgeteilt. Das britische Team brach früh zum jeweiligen Ort des Surveys auf. Nur einmal pro Woche konnte ich zum Informationsaustausch nach Homeh fahren. Die Kontakte zwischen den beiden europäischen Teams wurden vor allem von dem Arabisten Robert Hoyland und dem

Architekten Richard Anderson getragen (Taf. 35b). Gemeinsame Restaurantbesuche und Ausflüge zu nahe gelegenen Ruinenorten fanden in größeren Abständen statt (Taf. 35c). Erst am Ende jeder Kampagne trafen sich alle drei Gruppen beim Abschiedsfest in unserem Grabungshaus.

1997–2007. Probleme des Ruinenortes: Beduinenzelte, tausende von Schafen und Autopisten

Ich hatte schon einleitend darauf hingewiesen, dass die Beduinenstämme nicht anerkannten, dass Androna nicht mehr privat genutzt werden durfte. Nur für kurze Zeit wurde unser Kampf gegen hunderte von Schafen im Frühjahr im Ruinengelände, die Nutzung einzelner Räume der Ruinen für die Schafschur, die Errichtung von Zelten für Großfamilien im Frühjahr und vor allem gegen den Durchgangsverkehr der Autos quer durch den Ruinenort erfolgreich. Es war Abdelrassak Zaqzouq, der genug Erfahrungen mit der Nachbesiedlung des Ruinenortes hatte, der uns unterstützte hatte. Doch schon nach seinem Verzicht auf die Grabungsleitung nach nur einem Jahr blieb mir nur noch die Verhandlung mit einzelnen Beduinen – mit sehr unterschiedlichem Ergebnis.

So waren wir also gezwungen, am Grabungsende den Zugang zu freigelegten Räumen so gut es ging mit Steinen zu blockieren. Selbst die westliche Außenmauer des Kastrons wurde erst in den beiden letzten Kampagnen in voller Höhe freigelegt, um in Aufnahmen den Gesamteindruck des Baus festzuhalten (Taf. 22b). Keiner der drei Wächter schützte den Ort nach Grabungsende – die reichen Schafzüchter bestimmten die Regeln. Bei einer eventuellen Fortsetzung der Grabungsarbeiten in Androna wäre von Anfang an die Wohnsituation der Wächter so zu verbessern, dass sie nach Ende der Kampagnen am Grabungsort wohnen können.

Aussichtslos war der Kampf gegen den ständigen Autoverkehr durch den Ort und er blieb vergeblich, weil in den Institutionen in Hama zwar einige Maßnahmen diskutiert, aber keine einzige realisiert wurde.

2001. Autounfall vor Grabungsbeginn; Anschlag am 11. September 2001 in New York

Ich holte Anfang August den von zwei Mitarbeitern überführten Landrover Defender an der Grenzstation Bab al-Hawa ab. Wir fuhren über Aleppo nach Maslouchiye, einem Nachbarort von Androna. Wenige Kilometer vor Androna platzte der rechte hintere Reifen und das Auto stürzte, sich zweimal überschlagend, einen Abhang hinunter. Großes Glück: Die beiden Studenten waren nicht verletzt. Am Steuer saß die Mudira und sie kam mit mehrfachem Schleudertrauma und Hämatomen an Beinen und Armen ins Krankenhaus nach Aleppo. Am vierten Tag kam Hussein aus Qasr ibn Wardan mit einem Chauffeur – beide in blendend weißem Gewand – und ich wurde, bequem im Transporter liegend, nach Androna transportiert – wunderbar.

Als ich mit Halskrause und lädierten Beinen zum festlich geschmückten Grabungshaus kam, wurde ich von einem verjüngten Team empfangen: Ulrike Hess, die Grabungsarchitektin, hatte zu ihrer Unterstützung zwei junge Architekten aus München mitgebracht (Taf. 41b) – großartig. Trotz der enormen Probleme, die mit der ‚Entsorgung' des Unfallautos und meinem täglichen Kampf in Polizeistationen verbunden waren, war die Stimmung auf der Grabung fast heiter – wir hatten überlebt und alle waren hochmotiviert.

Das änderte sich mit dem Anschlag in New York am 11. September 2001. In allen Dörfern der Umgebung von Androna fanden Siegesfeiern statt. Da selbst mein langjähriger Mitarbeiter Ghassan die Siegesfeiern begrüßte, wurde dem ganzen Team überdeutlich der Abstand zwischen uns und allen, mit denen wir täglich in Kontakt waren, bewusst. Noch radikaler wirkten sich die Ereignisse auf das britische Team aus: Die negative Einstellung gegenüber Briten und Amerikanern war nun nicht mehr latent vorhanden, sondern brach offen aus. Die Grabungskampagne des Oxford-Teams wurde abgebrochen.

2002. Rückkehr von A. Sammakiya; Kultivierung der Ländereien im Umland von Androna

Nach dem Autounfall fiel im Folgejahr die Grabungskampagne des deutschen Teams aus. Vor unserer Rückkehr zur Kampagne im Sommer 2003 hatte die Ankunft von Adnan Sammakiya die Gesamtsituation von Androna verändert. Im Jahr 2002 war die von Felsbrocken durchsetzte Piste, die dorthin führte, in seinem Auftrag durch eine voll ausgebaute Asphaltstraße ersetzt worden. Vor dem westlichen Zugang zum Grabungsort bog die Straße ab zu dem großen Hauskomplex, den Sammakiya vor der Nordostseite von Androna errichten ließ (Taf. 36a. b). In nur einem Jahr waren ein Verwaltungshaus und mehrere traditionelle Bienenkorbhäuser als Wohnräume errichtet worden. Die luxuriöse Inneneinrichtung des Wohntrakts und vor allem das große Wasserbassin im Innenhof der Bauanlage waren nicht nur überraschend, sondern auch schockierend: In der wasserarmen Region ein offenes Becken, dessen Besitzer uns zum Schwimmen einlud (Taf. 36b): Welche Funktion hatte die mit viel Geld errichtete Anlage?

Adnan Sammakiya berichtete mir, dass er nach den Bestimmungen der Landreformen der Baath-Partei (1963–1966 und 1966–1970), die zu einem großen Teil die Nutzung seiner Ländereien betrafen, nach Kanada ausgewandert war. In den 1980er und 1990er Jahren waren die Gesetze für Landbesitz weitergehend geändert, die Staatsfarmen privatisiert und die Bestimmungen für Export und Import liberal gestaltet worden. Investoren wurden intensiv gefördert[46]. Dies waren die Veränderungen in Wirtschaft und Landwirtschaft, als Adnan Sammakiya als reicher Mann aus Kanada zurückkam.

Die Pläne von Adnan Sammakiya waren weitreichend und konzentrierten sich auf die Anlage von Plantagen auf den Ländereien der Familie. Für die Tropfenbewässerung der Pflanzen hatte er bis zu rund 700 m Tiefe nach Wasser graben lassen und war überzeugt, auf unterirdische Ströme gestoßen zu sein – eine Darstellung, die mich nicht überzeugte. Ich hatte 1997 ein Landgut besucht (Besitzer: Hasch Halul), das mit elektrischen Pumpen aus einem 500 m tiefen Brunnen bewässert wurde. Ich hielt es also für wahrscheinlicher, dass die kostbaren, sehr tief liegenden und uralten Wasserreservoire der Region angezapft wurden. Zu viele Dörfer hatte ich in Zentralsyrien gesehen, die nach maßloser Ausnutzung des Grundwassers mit elektrischen Pumpen aufgegeben werden mussten. Trotz meiner Skepsis verfolgte ich mit Spannung die fortschreitende Bepflanzung der Ländereien, da diese Arbeiten unmittelbar auf die Situation in Androna einwirkten.

Die Aktivitäten von Adnan Sammakiya betrafen die Ländereien vor der Nord- und Ostseite von Androna. Ein Mitglied der Familie Sammakiya hatte mir schon 1997 auf dem Plan mit dem Landbesitz der Familie gezeigt, dass die Ländereien im Norden und Osten bis vor die Mauern von Androna führten. Das britische Team hatte schon zu Beginn seines Surveys die Reste einer Stylitensäule freigelegt[47]. Sie war nur wenige Meter von der nördlichen Umfassungsmauer entfernt. Wie konnte das Umland von Androna geschützt werden?

Im Sommer 2003, ein Jahr nach dem Beginn seiner Pflanzungen, traf Adnan Sammakiya im Museum von Hama mit dem Bürgermeister und den Leitern der Grabungsteams zusammen. Ein Vertrag wurde aufgesetzt, der absichern sollte, dass die Ländereien vor der Nord- und Ostseite von Androna nicht Teil der landwirtschaftlichen Aktivitäten sein würden. Der Vertrag war auch nach 2007 noch nicht unterschrieben, doch die Ländereien östlich und nördlich des Ruinenortes blieben in dem vertraglich vorgeschriebenen Abstand frei. Das britische Team konnte seinen Survey fortsetzen.

Die erste negative Nachricht zum Verlauf des Projektes erreichte mich im Frühjahr 2004: Die große Anzahl schon gesetzter Pflanzen war, wie berichtet wurde, von Jugendlichen (?) aus den Dörfern der Region herausgerissen worden. Sie mussten neu gekauft und gesetzt werden. Die Stimmung hinter diesen Aktionen und die grundlegend negative Einstellung in der Region bekam während der Kampagne 2004 auch das deutsche Team mit: Die Familie Sammakiya lud das deutsche Team zum Essen ein, doch einige Mitglieder meines Teams wollten nicht mitgehen, da Arbeiter aus dem Dorf Sammakiya negativ über die Grundbesitzerfamilie berichtet hatten. Was war geschehen? Adnan Sammakiya hatte den jüngsten Sohn unserer Köchin für die Grundschule mit Schulranzen etc. ausgestattet, doch dieser weigerte sich zu gehen. Die Bezahlung der Köchin wurde als zu niedrig beurteilt und für die Arbeiten auf den Ländereien wurden keine Arbeiter aus Sammakiya eingestellt. Dass die in den 60er Jahren in ganz Syrien errichteten Grundschulen mit den obligatorischen Basketballkörben nur zu häufig nur von wenigen Grundschülern aufgesucht wurden, konnten wir beobachten. Und gut vorstellbar war, dass die Ablehnung der Familie, nach der der Ort Sammakiya benannt war, eine lange Vorgeschichte hatte. Auf meine Frage, wie hoch er die Arbeiten von Umm Saleh bezahlt hat, antwortete Adnan ausweichend: *„Nach den gängigen Sätzen"*.

Doch die Zerstörung der Pflanzen führte einerseits weit zurück zu dem traditionellen Kampf der Beduinenstämme gegen die landwirtschaftliche Nutzung von Ländereien und war andererseits eng mit den negativen Folgen der Landreformen in den vorangegangenen Jahrzehnten verbunden.

Schon vor Beginn der Grabung in Androna war ich häufig Gast der Familie des schon öfter erwähnten Scheichs von Qasr ibn Wardan (Taf. 10b). Sie bewohnte das nur wenige Schritte vom frühbyzantinischen Baukomplex entfernte Lehmziegelhaus der Antikenkommission. Abu Hussein blieb in allen Grabungskampagnen meine wichtigste Kontaktperson, obwohl er kein Befürworter der Arbeiten in Androna war. Als Vertreter einer Tradition, für die die Schafzucht an erster Stelle stand, übernahm er in jedem Jahr die Betreuung von ein paar hundert Schafen und wurde nach deren Verkauf am Gewinn beteiligt.

Ganz anders war die Situation von Chalid al Taki aus Sroudj, unserem wichtigsten Mitarbeiter: Der große Pickup, mit dem er jeden Tag die Arbeiter aus

Djenad abholte, war ihm von der Regierung gestellt worden und er hatte ihn über viele Jahre hin abzuzahlen. Den Zementtransport und die Fertigung der Zementsteine hatte er übernommen. Er errichtete aus Zementsteinen für seine Familie ein großes Haus, legte einen kleinen Olivenhain und Gemüsebeete an und nahm in seinem Dorf eine wichtige Stellung ein. Für Abu Hussein und seinen ältesten Sohn Hussein (Taf. 41a), der sich auf die Jagd und Ausbildung von Falken spezialisiert hatte, war die Bindung an die Regierung die Lösung von der Beduinentradition. Für den Jüngsten der Söhne des Scheichs war Chalid ein Vorbild, und er beneidete ihn um seine täglichen Aktivitäten und sein Einkommen. Im Gespräch mit Chalid erfuhr ich, dass dem Sohn von Abu Hussein leider das Startkapital für einen kleinen Laden an der Straße fehlte. Nach Rücksprache mit Abu Husein beschloss ich, ihm dieses Kapital als Vorauszahlung für künftige Arbeiten auf der Grabung zu zahlen – das war ein großer Fehler. Die Kosten für den Bau eines kleinen Ladens an der Straße waren nicht höher als ein neuer Raum am Grabungshaus von Androna. Er war schnell fertiggestellt, doch er blieb in den kommenden Jahren leer, da das Geld für die erste Verkaufsware nicht zusammenkam.

Wie zu erwarten war, hatte sich die ganze Geschichte in Windeseile herumgesprochen und nicht nur unsere Köchin erwartete eine Vorauszahlung für die Hochzeit ihres Sohnes, auch einige Arbeiter sahen in einer derartigen Vorfinanzierung ihres Lohnes in Androna eine Chance. Ich hatte einen Fehler gemacht und habe ihn in keinem der späteren Fälle korrigieren können.

2003. Fortsetzung der Grabung

Die nächste Kampagne fand erst 2003 statt: Zur Behandlung meiner Unfallschäden und mit endlich einmal viel Zeit für den Lehrbetrieb hatte ich die Kampagne abgesagt. Als ich im Juli 2003 zur Vorbereitung der Grabung nach Damaskus kam, erfuhr ich in der Generaldirektion, dass die beantragte Fortsetzung der so dringend erforderlichen geophysikalischen Aufnahmen nicht genehmigt worden war[48]. Die zweite Information kam aus dem Deutschen Archäologischen Institut in Damaskus: Für die Fernsehproduktion „*Schliemanns Erben*" wurde die Aufnahme der Grabung in Androna nicht nur empfohlen, sondern dringend nahegelegt. Die dritte Information war wichtig für alle kommenden Arbeiten in Androna: Die Einführung und weite Verbreitung von Handys hatten das Straßenbild nicht nur in Damaskus verändert. Die Anschaffung und der Gebrauch von Handys waren so günstig, dass Ghassan auch mich sofort ausstattete und darauf vorbereitete, dass ich alle Grabungsmitarbeiter mit einem Handy antreffen würde. Vor der Weiterreise nach Androna konnte ich die Neuplanung der Grabungskampagne bei der Antikenkommission einreichen. Ich kam nach Homeh auf die Asphaltstraße, die zum Haus von Adnan Sammakiya führte. Mein erster Gedanke war: Hätte es sie doch schon 2001 gegeben, als ich mit Halskrause und lädierten Beinen unter jedem Schlag auf der miserablen Piste gelitten hatte. Und der zweite Gedanke führte zurück in das Nordsyrische Kalksteinmassiv, wo nach dem Bau vieler kleiner Asphaltstraßen im Rahmen des Programms zur Förderung des Tourismus der Antikenraub zugenommen hatte. Pickups konnten dort nun direkt vor die Kirchen fahren und aufladen, was gut verkäuflich erschien. Die schlechte Piste hatte den Weg nach Androna erschwert, die Asphaltstraße dagegen steigerte den Durchgangsverkehr und erleichterte den Abtransport interessanter Objekte. Ich stellte also sofort eine Liste all der Objekte auf, die am Ende jeder Kampagne in das Museum in Hama gebracht werden sollten.

Die Grabungsarbeiten hatten gerade begonnen, als vom Deutschen Archäologischen Institut die Nachricht kam, in wenigen Tagen würde ein Fernsehteam am Ruinenort eintreffen. Rückfragen zur Aufnahme des britischen und des syrischen Teams in die Dokumentation blieben ohne Antwort. Ich konnte mich nur damit trösten, dass das britische Team kein Interesse an einer Beteiligung hatte, da es den Survey außerhalb von Androna begonnen hatte. Die Verbindung der Grabungsarbeiten mit den Dreharbeiten wurde trotz aller Probleme irgendwie bewältigt und wir hatten schon ein rauschendes Abschiedsfest vorbereitet, als mich ein Anruf aus der Antikenverwaltung zu unmöglich früher Zeit nach Damaskus beorderte. Es war nicht nur der harsche Ton, in dem mir mitgeteilt wurde, dass im nächsten Jahr Restaurierungsarbeiten in Androna durchzuführen seien, es war vor allem das damit verbundene Verbot von Grabungsarbeiten während der Restaurierung.

Ich fuhr nach dem deprimierenden Gespräch in der Generaldirektion Syrischer Altertümer vollkommen erledigt nach Androna zurück und begann schon unterwegs, Wege zur Umgehung des Grabungsverbots und zur Finanzierung der Restaurierung anzudenken. Während des Abschiedsfests mit dem Filmteam konnte ich weder meinen Mitarbeitern noch dem Leiter der Dreharbeiten meine triste Stimmung erklären – alle eventuellen Lösungen hingen noch ungeklärt in der Luft. Erst nach der Ankunft in Damaskus am Ende der Grabungskampagne konnte ich mit Karin Bartl, der Leiterin des DAI, diskutieren, für welche ausgegrabenen Räume des Kastrons, des Hauses und der Außenmauer eine Restaurierung zu einem so frühen Zeitpunkt sinnvoll sein könnte, und welche Möglichkeiten der Finanzierung es gab. Mein Antrag auf Unterstützung der Restaurierung beim Auswärtigen Amt wurde bewilligt und ich hatte nur noch einen Plan auszuarbeiten, der in Damaskus akzeptiert werden konnte.

2004. Restaurierungsarbeiten in Androna

Im Zentrum der Restaurierungsarbeiten im August 2004 stand der Westtrakt des Kastrons: das Westtor mit den flankierenden Türmen und das hoch anstehende Rampenhaus – überwiegend in Basalt konstruiert (Taf. 27a. b). Für die in Lehmziegeln in Verbindung mit Basaltelementen errichteten Räume des Hauskomplexes (Taf. 25a) sowie das Nordtor der Außenmauer hatte ich als vorläufige Maßnahme, d. h. bis zur detaillierten zeichnerischen Aufnahme, die Sicherung der Lehmziegelmauern durch gebrannte Ziegel aus dem Kastron vorgeschlagen. Für die schwierige Restaurierung des Westtors wurde ein Team der TU Potsdam gewonnen (Taf. 39b), und die Antikenkommission stellte den größten vorhandenen Kran zur Verfügung (Taf. 27). Die Bearbeitung von Basaltquadern, mit denen die oberen Quaderlagen der Türme und des Rampenhauses restauriert wurden, lag in den Händen von Abu Mohammed aus Suweida.

Dankbar war ich für die Unterstützung bei allen Fragen zur Planung und Durchführung der Restaurierung durch Medjd Hjazi, Mitarbeiter am Museum von Hama, und Waʿal al Haffian, dem Kommissar auf der Kampagne im Jahr 2003 (Taf. 38b).

Die Fortsetzung von Grabungsarbeiten durch Freilegung des Vestibüls, das zum Innenhof des Kastrons führte (Taf. 25a), hatte ich mit dem von der Antikenverwaltung gewünschten ‚Sightseeing-Plan' für Touristen begründet. Zum Glück konnte kein offizieller Vertreter der Antikenverwaltung in Damaskus den Umfang dieser Freilegungsarbeiten einschätzen, da bis 2004 noch keiner die Grabung besucht hatte.

Nach Abschluss der Restaurierungen im Kastron und im Hauskomplex wurden für die letzten beiden Kampagnen neue Schwerpunkte entwickelt: Im Kastron begann die Freilegung und Gesamtaufnahme der Kirche des Innenhofes (Taf. 32c), im Haus wurde die Untersuchung des Innenhofes und der Wohnräume an seiner Nordseite aufgenommen, die zweite Torgrabung der Außenmauer wurde begonnen und der Gesamtplan der Siedlung wurde ab 2004 durch Höhenvermessungen im gesamten Ruinenort ergänzt[49].

Der Neuorientierung gingen personelle Veränderungen im Grabungsteam voraus, die eine Zäsur im Gesamtablauf des Grabungsprojektes darstellten. Als im Frühjahr 2007 das alte Grabungsteam noch einmal zu Nacharbeiten am Grabungsort zusammentraf, war allen bewusst, dass sich die Filmaufnahmen und vor allem die Restaurierungsarbeiten auf das Gesamtprogramm so auswirkten, dass im Rückblick die Arbeiten der Jahre 1997–2001 einen Schwerpunkt darstellten.

2005. Situation der Hausgrabung nach der Freilegung eines Bodenmosaiks

Als bei der Hausgrabung 2005 ein großartiges Bodenmosaik freigelegt wurde, war sofort klar, dass es nicht am Ort bleiben konnte (Taf. 25b). Über das Museum in Hama wurde ein auf Bodenmosaiken spezialisiertes Team aus Maʿarret en Nomʿan nach Androna gerufen, und vor dem Ende der Grabungskampagne war der Transport zum Museum in Hama bewältigt. Es kamen Besucher aus den umliegenden Dörfern und selbst aus Hama und Aleppo. Zum ersten Mal erlebte ich auf der Grabung, dass die lokalen Mitarbeiter sich über einen Grabungsfund unterhielten: *"So ein Mosaik kostet viel, der Mann war wohlhabend"*. Ich hatte in den vorangegangenen Kampagnen nicht vermitteln können, dass die Bauten, die freigelegt wurden, Teil ihrer Geschichte sind.

Nach dem Auftauchen des Mosaiks läuteten bei mir sofort die Alarmglocken. Das Interesse an ‚Hausgrabungen' würde in den Monaten der Abwesenheit des Grabungsteams zunehmen. Zu tief hatte mich die Erfahrung mit Raubgrabungen geprägt. Doch nach den Ereignissen in den Jahren nach 2011 kann ich auch in dem Transport ins Museum von Hama keine Lösung sehen: Wir wissen nichts über seinen Zustand nach der Plünderung des Museums.

2006. Ausgrabung der Kastronkirche; Feier des ‚Tages der Wüste / Steppe' im Frühjahr

Als ich im Juli 2006 zur Vorbereitung der Grabung nach Androna kam, traf ich im Zentrum des Ortes zahlreiche Glasscherben und Fragmente chemischer Toiletten an. Diese ‚Überreste' und die Reifenspuren von Autos und Motorrädern auf den Haushügeln waren ein großer Schock. Die Antikenwächter berichteten, dass im April der ‚Tag der Wüste / Steppe' nicht wie üblich in Qasr ibn Wardan, sondern in Androna stattgefunden hatte. Für zahlreiche geladene Gäste, die sich mit ihren Autos im Zentrum versammelt hatten, seien zwanzig Schafe geschlachtet worden, die Adnan Sammakiya gestiftet hatte. Keiner von ihnen, den Antikenwächtern, sei eingeladen gewesen, doch sie hätten hinterher, so gut es ging, aufgeräumt.

Der Bürgermeister von Hama habe zur Feier des Festes eine Broschüre über Androna herausgegeben und sie hätten ein Exemplar für mich aufgehoben (Taf. 32). Die lokalen Mitarbeiter unserer Grabung gaben mir das Heft, nachdem sie es vorher demonstrativ zerknautscht hatten. Die Broschüre zeigte eine Ansicht von Qasr ibn Wardan auf der Titelseite (Taf. 32a) und enthielt einige Farbfotos vom Westtrakt des Kastrons. Auf einen einleitenden Text des Bürgermeisters von Hama folgte ein englischer Text von Marlia Mango und ein deutscher Text von mir. Überraschend war allein eines der Farbfotos (Taf. 32b): Eine Montage zeigte den Syrischen Präsidenten Baschar al Assad auf einem Sessel sitzend in der Öffnung des Westtors.

Die Überreste des Wüstenfestes und die Spuren der Autos hatten eine Vorgeschichte. Ich hatte den Museumsdirektor und den Bürgermeister von Hama 2003 mit dem Gesamtplan von Androna aufgesucht, in dem alle kreuz und quer durch den Ruinenort führenden Autopisten eingezeichnet waren und um Unterstützung beim Kampf gegen den Durchgangsverkehr gebeten. Die zahlreichen Besucher des Wüstenfestes hatten ihre Autos nicht außen, sondern im Zentrum von Androna geparkt – deutlicher hätte die Reaktion auf meine Bitte nicht ausfallen können.

Die Kommentare meines Grabungsteams zu dem Foto des syrischen Präsidenten waren damals durchgehend negativ: *„Das hat das Westtor nicht verdient".* Ich konnte mich 2006 nicht lösen von den Erfahrungen, die ich in Hama gemacht hatte: Bei der Auffahrt zum Luxushotel, erbaut nach der Zerstörung der Altstadt, wies mich Abdelrassak Zaqzouq auf die Ruinen der Altstadthäuser rechts der Auffahrt hin, die – wie er informierte – bewusst stehen gelassen wurden. In jeder Familie, in der ich in Hama zu Gast war, wurde mit Trauer zurückgeblickt – die Ereignisse von 1982 waren nicht vergessen.

Situation der Kirche im Hof des Kastrons

Kein Ausgrabungsplatz in Androna war bei den Arbeitern aus Djenad so unbeliebt wie die Kirche im Hof des Kastrons (Taf. 32c). Nachdem 2005 die Schuttberge im Inneren ausgeräumt worden waren, mussten wir bei den Grabungsarbeiten feststellen, dass der gesamte Innenraum mithilfe eines Baggers so weitgehend zerstört worden war, dass wir nur wenige Zentimeter des originalen

Kirchenbodens vorfanden. Ich wunderte mich, dass man selbst die Säulenbasen ausgegraben und abtransportiert hatte. War geplant worden, im Inneren Gemüse, Kartoffeln oder was auch immer anzupflanzen? Ein Arbeiter klärte mich auf: Säulenbasen lassen sich gut verkaufen. Sie werden beim Bau neuer Häuser eingesetzt. Womit auch dieses Rätsel gelöst war!

Zur tristen Stimmung am Ende der Kampagne trug auch der Bericht von Nasser, dem Vorarbeiter des Teams aus Djenad bei: Die staatliche Subvention für Dünger und Dieseltreibstoff, notwendig für das Betreiben der Grundwasserpumpen, war eingestellt worden. Da viele Kleinbauern in der Wasserversorgung auf elektrische Pumpen angewiesen waren, hatte sich mit dieser Veränderung ihre wirtschaftliche Situation deutlich verschlechtert. Die Probleme wurden noch verschärft durch eine Dürre infolge der geringen Regenfälle in den Wintermonaten.

Nach dem Ende der Kampagne 2006 sprach ich mit dem Bürgermeister über das Wüstenfest und fragte nach der Fotomontage in seiner Broschüre. Er sprach davon, dass nun nach Qasr ibn Wardan auch Androna ein wichtiges Reiseziel sei, und seine Broschüre liege im Museum für Touristen aus. Auf meine Frage nach dem Foto ging er nicht ein.

2007. Kampagne der Fundbearbeitung

Im April 2007 trafen sich Mitglieder des alten Grabungsteams zusammen mit dem Architekten Oliver Hofmeister zur Fundbearbeitung in Androna. Als Leihauto wurde ausgerechnet ein alter VW-Käfer organisiert (Taf 33a b) – ich kam in das Auto weder richtig rein, noch ohne Probleme wieder heraus.

Zur guten Stimmung während dieser Kampagne trug der Besuch aus Damaskus bei: Abdal Rasssak Moaz, Generaldirektor der Antikenkommission, hatte viel Zeit für die Besichtigung des Kastrons und der frühharabischen Badanlage mitgebracht. Er blieb bis zum Abschiedstreffen, das mit frischen Champignons aus den Lehmziegelhügeln der Hausgrabung (Taf. 34b), der am ganzen Ort wachsenden Rucola, weißen Trüffeln aus Aleppo (Taf. 34a) und herrlichen Frühlingsblumen gefeiert wurde.

Positiv waren 2007 auch die Informationen von Adnan Sammakiya: Die Rekultivierung der Ländereien war abgeschlossen. Ich wurde eingeladen, an der ersten Ernte teilzunehmen, die in circa zwei Jahren erwartet wurde. Mich hatte Adnans Gesamtprogramm von Anfang an fasziniert – trotz der ungeklärten

Wasserversorgung und trotz der Spannungen, die es in den Nachbardörfern von Androna und selbst in meinem Grabungsteam hervorgerufen hatte.

2010. Erste Kampagne in der Hauptkirche von Androna

Unter der Grabungsleitung von Fedor Schlimbach hatte 2010 die erste Kampagne zur Erforschung der Hauptkirche Andronas begonnen. Im Sommer 2011 kam aus der Antikenkommission die Nachricht, dass der Antikenwächter des deutschen Teams wegen Steinraubs entlassen worden war. Ich schlug als Nachfolger Mohammed, den Sohn von Scheich Ibrahim vor. Die damals noch nicht geschlossene Vertretung des Deutschen Archäologischen Instituts in Damaskus überwies das Geld für die Bezahlung des neuen Wächters. Das Wächtergeld konnte so bis 2013 überwiesen werden, doch nach der Schließung der Abteilung und der veränderten Situation der Banken in Syrien wurde sie eingestellt.

Der Grund für die Kündigung des Wächters war für mich nach meinen Erfahrungen nicht überraschend: Er hatte das große Lager an Mauersteinen aus den Kastrongrabungen – es waren etwas über 9000 Basaltsteine – „abtransportiert". Mir war bewusst, dass dieser Steinraub mehrere Pickups und eine größere Gruppe von Mitarbeitern erfordert hatte, und dass an der Aktion nicht nur der Wächter beteiligt war.

Die Arbeiten in der Hauptkirche konnten nach der ersten Kampagne nicht fortgesetzt werden[50].

2016. Zerstörungen durch den IS im Kastron von Androna

Im Sommer 2018 war die Journalistin Karin Leukefeld, begleitet von syrischem Militär, in Androna und schickte mir Aufnahmen von den Zerstörungen durch den IS im Jahr 2016 (Taf. 28–31). Sie hielt sich mit ihrer Begleitung ausschließlich im Zentrum des Ortes auf, da eine Rundfahrt durch den ganzen Ort zu gefährlich war. Die Ruine des Grabungshauses wurde nur aus größerer Distanz fotografiert und mit wenigen Aufnahmen die Situation der Hauptkirche und der beiden Badanlagen erfasst. Der Verfall des Grabungshauses war 2016 schon weit fortgeschritten, weil in den Jahren nach der letzten Kampagne eines deutschen Grabungsteams im Jahr 2010 die großen Eisentüren und die Fenster ausgebaut und verkauft worden waren.

Die Mitglieder der al Nusra und des IS wohnten 2015 sehr wahrscheinlich nicht im Grabungshaus, sondern in den luxuriös ausgestatteten *Trulli* vor der

Nordostecke von Androna (Taf. 36a). Adnan Sammakiya hatte nach der Entführung seines jüngsten Sohnes und der Freilassung nach Bezahlung des Lösegeldes seinen Wohnkomplex und die Ländereien schon vor 2015 verlassen. In einem Telefonat mit seinem ältesten Sohn erfuhr ich 2019, dass er nicht wisse, in welchem Zustand die Plantagen sind.

Alle detaillierten Aufnahmen von Karin Leukefeld konzentrierten sich 2018 und 2019 auf das Kastron. Auch ohne Kenntnis des Ruinenortes und der Aktivitäten der Grabungsteams war sofort erkennbar, dass die Zerstörungen den Westtrakt des Kastrons betrafen. Die Toranlage an der Südseite des Kastrons war unbeschädigt. Ein arabischer Schriftzug auf dem Turm vor der Südseite des Westtores hält fest, dass die ‚Freien Damaszener' für die Zerstörungen verantwortlich sind.

Das Westtor (Taf. 29) und alle hoch anstehenden Teile der westlichen Eingangsanlage, des Rampenhauses, der Westhalle (Taf. 30b) der Latrine und der Südhalle (Taf. 31) wurden mit Dynamit gesprengt. Da sie in einem Schichtmauerwerk aus Basaltquadern und gebrannten Ziegeln errichtet worden waren, musste mit den Dynamitladungen wohl bei jedem Raum neu angesetzt werden. Die noch teilweise erhaltenen Basaltlagen lassen erkennen, dass die Zerstörungen sich auf den Zugang zum Hof des Kastrons, den Eingang in das Rampenhaus und den Weg über die Rampenläufe zu den oberen Geschossen, die Türen in die großen Hallen und die hoch anstehende Nordwand der Südhalle (Taf. 31a. b) konzentrierten. Die Aufnahme eines Schuttberges mit dem Fragment einer der Basalttüren (Taf. 31c) zeigt, dass keine der Türen – ausgenommen das Westtor – restauriert werden kann.

Die Zerstörung des 2004 restaurierten Haupttores war nicht nur ein Schock. Sie bleibt schmerzhaft bis zur erneuten Restaurierung des Tores. Der Sturz mit der berühmten Stifterinschrift liegt zusammen mit dem Innensturz in der Toröffnung. Die Tatsachen, dass die Kreuzmonogramme auf beiden Stürzen nicht abgearbeitet wurden, die zweite große Toranlage an der Südseite des Kastrons nicht gesprengt wurde und die Aktivitäten des IS weder die Kirche im Innenhof des Kastrons (Taf. 32c) noch die Hauptkirche von Androna erfassten, werfen einige Fragen auf. Der Sturz des Westtores war – trotz der circa sechs Meter hohen Verschüttungslagen des Kastrons (Taf. 22a) – auch vor der vollständigen Freilegung des Tores über Jahrhunderte sichtbar geblieben. Doch das wirkliche Wahrzeichen von Androna war und ist bis heute der circa zehn Meter hoch anstehende Rest des Apsisbogens der Hauptkirche.

Das zweite Projekt: Grabungsarbeiten in al-Andarin, dem antiken Androna

Die Fragen führten zurück zu der Broschüre, die der Bürgermeister von Hama 2006 publiziert hatte. Die Übersetzung des vom Bürgermeister verfassten Textes in der Broschüre, die ich anfertigen ließ[51], führte in eine nicht erwartete Richtung. Der Text beschreibt die Lage und den byzantinischen Ursprung des Ortes, nennt die letzte Erwähnung des Ortes im Jahr 1225 durch den Geographen Yakut al-Hamawi[52] und verbindet das große Erbe der Wüste mit dem Ruhm des Weines von al Andarin in der Mo´allaqat des Amr[53]. Die letzte Botschaft zum Fest der Wüste lautet: „*Der heutige Aufstieg der Umma (der Nation?), trotz der Härte der von den Arabern erfahrenen Umstände, hat den Fortschritt und die Entwicklung unserer Nation nicht verlangsamt. Indem wir den Fußstapfen von Bashar al-Assad folgen, dem Präsidenten der Arabischen Syrischen Republik, werden wir zum Vorbild der Nation, die ihren alten Ruhm aufgebaut hat und den Aufbau ihrer neuen Zivilisation vorantreiben wird. Noch einmal heißen wir Sie willkommen in Hama*".

Für die Gäste des Wüstenfestes war die Broschüre ein positiv gemeinter Willkommensgruß. Meine Frage nach dem Bild Assads in der Öffnung des Westtores ist dennoch nicht klar beantwortet. Mit der Verlegung des Wüstenfestes von Qasr ibn Wardan nach Androna wurde zwar die Bedeutung des Ruinenortes anerkannt. Doch war dem Bürgermeister klar, wie die Reaktion der Mitarbeiter der Grabung auf die ganze Aktion sein würde? Es ist schwer vorstellbar, dass Mitglieder des IS die Broschüre aus dem Museum mitgenommen haben. Für die Mitglieder des Islamischen Staats war die Sprengung des Westtors in Androna eine von vielen Aktionen, die darauf zielten, so weitgehend wie möglich das kulturelle Erbe Syriens zu zerstören. Die Annahme, dass die Aktion in Androna irgendwie mit der Broschüre zu tun hatte, die unter den Grabungsmitarbeitern kursierte, ist eine nicht beweisbare Vermutung.

Überlegungen zur ‚*Syrians for Heritage Association*' und dem ‚*Syrian Heritage Archive Projekt*'

Eine der Motivationen für meine jahrelangen Arbeiten im Nordsyrischen Kalksteinmassiv war die Erfahrung mit Antikenraub. Ich traf ihn über viele Jahre hin – begleitet von Steinraub und Raubgrabungen – an allen antiken Orten an, in denen ich tätig war. Die Zerstörungen in al-Andarin / Androna durch den Islamischen Staat im Jahr 2016 haben dann alles übertroffen, was ich bis 2007 erlebt hatte – die gezielte Zerstörung des reichen kulturellen Erbes traf nach 2011 zahlreiche antike Stätten Syriens[54].

"In truth, Syria has always suffered – and the regime always tolerated – a limited amount of theft from historical sites, to boost the economy of in the poor areas in the north of the country and to enrich the regimes own mafiosi. But what is happening now is on a epic and terrifying scale" [55].

In dem Programm der ‚Syrians for heritage association', die im Januar 2018 in Berlin gegründet wurde, heißt es: *„Through our cultural heritage we can comprehend our past and anticipate our future. It helps us to rediscover our plurality, restore our sense of belonging to our land and country, and achieve our hoped-for peaceful future"*.

Die Berichte über das Nordsyrische Kalksteinmassiv haben gezeigt, dass keine zivile Institution existiert, die das Werk der Zerstörung aufhalten könnte. Ebenso ist offen, ob durch zukünftige Verbesserung der personellen Ausstattung der Antikendienste der perfekt organisierte und brutal agierende Antikenraub – wie auch intensive Raubgrabungen und Steinraub – wenigstens teilweise eingeschränkt werden können. Zu groß sind die Probleme der Restaurierung, die in Friedenszeiten auf alle an Syriens Kulturerbe Interessierte zukommen werden.

Die Aufnahme der Verluste, die Archivierung des noch Bestehenden und des in älteren Fotos und Zeichnungen Bewahrten hat begonnen. In einem großen Projekt der Universität Paris Nanterre werden alle älteren Aufnahmen zum Pilgerzentrum Qalʿat Simʿan unter der Leitung der Archäologin Micheline Kurdy archiviert[56]. Den zahlreichen Fragen der Digitalisierung und der Vermittlung der entstandenen Datenbanken innerhalb und außerhalb Syriens widmet sich das ‚Syrian Heritage Archive Projekt'[57]. Als vorläufig einzig möglichen Beitrag zu den international laufenden Arbeiten zur Erstellung umfassender Datenbanken habe ich die Materialien meiner Projekte in dem Institut meines Fachbereichs an der Universität Göttingen archiviert und zugänglich gemacht.

Abschließend komme ich auf die eingangs gestellte Frage nach dem Sinn von circa zwanzig Jahren Tätigkeit im Nordsyrischen Kalksteinmassiv und in einem der größten Ruinenorte Zentralsyriens zurück. Mit der umfangreichen Dokumentation von Fotos und Zeichnungen zu Elementen der Baudekoration kann das in zahlreichen Ruinenorten nicht mehr Vorhandene ergänzt werden. Dabei geht es nicht um das eine oder andere Kapitell – ach, schon wieder ein Kapitell – sondern um ein Charakteristikum der sogenannten ‚Toten Städte': Das überragende Können lokaler Werkstätten und Werkgruppen und ihr Kontakt zu den großen syrischen Stätten, in deren Einflussbereich das Bergmassiv liegt.

Das zweite Projekt: Grabungsarbeiten in al-Andarin, dem antiken Androna

Anders ist die Situation in al-Andarin, dem antiken Androna. Dort waren die an der Oberfläche greifbaren Einzelobjekte so weitgehend ausgeraubt, dass die Aufklärung über die Geschichte des Ortes nur durch Freilegung unter Erd- und Sandschichten begrabener Bauten zu erwarten war. Die Grabungsarbeiten im Kastron und in den beiden Badanlagen waren nicht nur reich an Ergebnissen für die frühbyzantinische Zeit – dem 4. bis frühen 7. Jahrhundert –, sie erbrachten auch weitreichende Informationen zur Nachnutzung des Ortes in früharabischer Zeit im frühen 7. und 8. Jahrhundert. Darüber hinaus konnten durch die hervorragende Arbeit des britischen Teams das antike Bewässerungssystem und die Grundlagen von Wirtschaft und Handel rekonstruiert werden.

Ich habe in meinem Bericht die Probleme und notwendigen Veränderungen angesprochen, die vor einer eventuellen Fortsetzung von Grabungsarbeiten in Androna zu lösen wären. Es wäre jedoch grotesk, darüber hinaus gehende Empfehlungen zur Wiederaufnahme der Grabungen in Androna vorzustellen – angesichts der immer noch verzweifelten Lage der Menschen in Syrien.

Anmerkungen

1   Strube 2019, 67–75.

2   SIMAT, Documenting the Current Condition of Saint Simeon Castle Damages and Violations, Report 2017-2020.

3   A. Kilb, Trost aus Trümmern, FAZ 2016, 1-2; K. Leukefeld, Aleppo – die geschundene Stadt atmet noch, Neues Deutschland, 4. Mai 2017, 3.

4   Bell 1905 / 2015; R. Lefèvre, Ashes of Hama. The Muslim Brotherhood in Syria, London 2013.

5   Butler 1920, *passim*.

6   Strube 2015, I-II, *passim*.

7   Butler 1920, *passim*.

8   Tchalenko 1953, *passim*.

9   Tchalenko 1980-1990, *passim*.

10 Loosley Leeming – Tchalenko 2019, 1-26.

11 Butler 1920, 48 erwähnt Raubgrabungen. Tchalenko 1953, I, 16 erwähnt das nicht weit von Androna entfernte Tell Minnis als Zentrum organisierten Antikenraubs. Charakteristisch ist der Passus bei Lassus über den Raub antiker Kapitelle für Neubauten (Lassus 1935–36, I, 207).

12 Bell 1905 / 2015, 266.

13 Strube 1993, 94-115.

14 Loosley Leeming – Tchalenko 2019, fig. 1.19.

15 S. Böhme, Männer jagen, Frauen sammeln, Berlin – Tübingen 2012, 194.

16 Butler 1929, 98.

17 Tchalenko 1953 I, 233f.; Strube 1993, 270.

18 Ch. Strube, Georges Tchalenko, Églises syriennes à bêma, Jahrbuch für Antike und Christentum 35, 1992, 222-228; Ch. Strube: Nachruf Georges Tchalenko, Gnomon 60, 1988, 667-668.

19 Strube 1993, 143-197; Strube 2002, 157-164.

20 de Vogüé 1865–1877, Taf. 62.

21 Ch. Strube, Die „Toten Städte". Stadt und Land in Nordsyrien während der Spätantike, Zaberns Bildbände zur Archäologie, Mainz 1996, 48 Abb. 84.

22 Strube 1993, 65-68, Taf. 35a. b.

23 Strube 2002, 5-16.

24 Strube 2002, Abb. 1a-l. 2a-g.

25 Strube 2002, 61 ff. 79 ff. Taf. 51.

26 Die Ausstellung „*Land des Baal, Syrien – Forum der Völker und Kulturen*" wurde von Eva Strommenger organisiert und begann 1982 in Berlin in der Großen Orangerie des Schlosses Charlottenburg.

27 Strube 2002, Taf. 22.

28 J.-P. Fourdrin, Église E.5 d'El Bara, Syria 69, 1992, 170-210.

29 SIMAT, Syrians for Heritage, Documenting the Current Condition of Saint Simeon Castle Damages and Violations, 2017-2020, 1-22. Die Fotos der Zerstörungen wurden mir großzügig für meine Publikation zur Verfügung gestellt.

30 *ibid.* 11.

31 Siehe Strube 2015, 198. 211-213. Vergleichbar ist die Situation in der Kirche des Kastrons von Androna: Nach der kompletten Ausraubung des Innenraumes wurden auch noch die Säulenbasen ausgegraben.

32 Dazu ausführlich Strube 1993, 209-217. 241-244. 267-270; Strube 2002, 215-225. Siehe auch die weiterführende Stellungnahme von B. Bavant, Les églises du Massif Calcaire de Syrie du Nord (VIe–VIIe s.), Journal of Roman Archaeology 2, 2005, 756-770.

33 Strube 1993, 205 Anm. 1135.

34 Loosly Leeming – Tchalenko 2019, 26. Der Beitrag der Koautorin ist mehr als problematisch und dies nicht nur wegen ihrer Probleme mit der deutschsprachigen Literatur.

35 Strube 2015, I-II, *passim*.

36 Schlimbach 2020, Taf. 8a.

37 Strube 1993, *passim*.

38 Butler 1920, 8-10.

39 D. Zevenhuizen, Land, Conflict and Agriculture in Syria, Wageningen University, Wageningen 2016, 11-27.

40 Mango 2010, 245–290, 245-270.

41 Strube 2015, I, 273 und 291f.

42 Strube 2015, I, 87-194.

43 Die Arbeiten wurden nach zwei Kampagnen eingestellt.

44 Strube 2015, I, 69-85.

45 Strube 2015, I, 192-220.

46 Zevenhuizen 2016 (s. o. Anm. 39), 14-19.

47 Mango 2010, 245–290, 274 f. fig. 28. 38.

48 Strube 2015, I, 56-60; Abb. 15.

49 Strube 2015, II, Plan 3.

50 Schlimbach 2020.

51 Ich danke Liana Saif für die Übersetzung des sprachlich schwierigen Textes.

52 Zu Yakut al Halawi siehe Strube 2015, I, 7.

53 Die Verse des Amr ibn Kultum (gest. 584) rühmen den Wein von Androna: „*Ha girl! Up with the bowl! Give us our dawn draught and do not spare the wines of Andarine*", dazu Strube 2015, I, 7 f.

54 R. Fisk, Syria's ancient treasures pulverised, Independent, 5. August 2012, 1-4.

55 *ibid.* 3-4.

56 Micheline Kurdy, Numérisation et accès aux archives archéologiques du site de Saint-Syméon. Das Projekt ist in die Fondation Aleph, die ‚Alliance internationale pour la protection du patrimoine dans les zones de conflits' integriert.

57 Issam Ballouz, Die digitale Rettung des syrischen Kulturerbes: Grenzen und Chancen, Syrian Heritage Archive Projekt, 2017, 66-74.

Literaturverzeichnis

Bell 1905: G. Bell, Am Ende des Lavastroms. Durch die Wüsten und Kulturstätten Syriens (1905). Hrsg. G. Habinger, Wien 2015.

Butler 1920: H. C. Butler, Syria. Publications of the Princeton University Archaeological Expeditions to Syria in 1904-5. Division II: Architecture, Section B: Northern Syria, Leyden 1920.

Butler 1929: H. C. Butler, Early churches in Syria, Princeton 1929.

Lassus 1935-36: J. Lassus, Inventaire archéologique de la région au nord-est de Hama. Documents d'études orientales IV, Band I-II. Damaskus 1935-1936.

Loosely Lemming – Tchalenko 2019: E. Loosely Lemming – J. Tchalenko, Symeon Stylites at Qalʿat Simʿān, Text and Studies in Eastern Christianity, Vol. XII, Leiden 2019.

Mango 2010: M. M. Mango, Androna in Syria: Questions of environment and economy, in: F. Daim – J. Drauschke (Hrsg.), Byzanz. Das Römerreich im Mittelalter 2, 1: Schauplätze. Monographien RGZM 84, 2, 1, Mainz 2010, 245-290.

Mouterde – Poidebard 1945: R. Mouterde – A. Poidebard, Le Limes de Chalkis. Organisation de la steppe en Haute-Syrie Romaine, Paris 1945.

Naccache 1992: A. Naccache, Le décor des églises de villages d'Antiochène du IVe au VIIe siècle, Paris 1992.

Schlimbach 2020: F. Schlimbach, Neue Forschungen in al-Andarīn. Das Ensemble der ‚Hauptkirche' von *Androna*, Heidelberg 2020.

Strube 1977: Ch. Strube, Die Formgebung der Apsisdekoration in Qalbloze und Qalat Siman, Jahrbuch für Antike und Christentum 20, 1977, 181-191.

Strube 1983: Ch. Strube, Die Kapitelle von Qasr ibn Wardan, Jahrbuch für Antike und Christentum 26, 1983, 59-106.

Strube 1993: Ch. Strube, Baudekoration im Nordsyrischen Kalksteinmassiv I. Kapitell-, Tür- und Gesimsformen des 4. und 5. Jahrhunderts n. Chr., Damaszener Forschungen 5, Mainz 1993.

Strube 2002: Ch. Strube, Baudekoration im Nordsyrischen Kalksteinmassiv II. Das 6. und frühe 7. Jahrhundert, Damaszener Forschungen 11, Mainz 2002.

Strube 2010: Ch. Strube, Al Andarin, das antike Androna, in: F. Daim – J. Drauschke (Hrsg.), Byzanz. Das Römerreich im Mittelalter 2, 1: Schauplätze. Monographien RGZM 84, 2, 1, Mainz 2010, 211-243.

Strube 2015, I-II: Ch. Strube, Al Andarin, das antike Androna. Oberflächenbefunde und Grabungsergebnisse: Die Umfassungsmauern und das Kastron, Monographie des RGZM 121, Mainz 2015.

Strube 2019: Ch. Strube, Das antike Androna. Zerstörungen durch den IS in Al Andarin, Antike Welt 3.19, 2019, 67-75.

Tchalenko 1953, I-III: G. Tchalenko, Villages antiques de la Syrie du Nord. Institut Français de Beyrouth, Bibliothèque archéologique et historique 50, volume I-III, Paris 1953.

Tchalenko 1980-1990: G. Tchalenko, Églises syriennes à bêma, I Texte (1990), II Planches (1979), III Album (1980).

de Vogüé 1865-1877, I-II: M. de Vogüé, Syrie centrale: Architecture civile et religieuse du Ier au VIIe siècle, 2 Bde. Paris 1865–1877.

As an Archaeologist in Syria

Experiences and Events

1971–1980 and 1997–2007

Preface

In 2016–2020, the Syrians for Heritage Association provided information about bombings by fighter planes, shell and rocket impacts, illegal excavations, stone theft and antiquities theft with reports and photos on the situation in Qalʿat Simʿan and numerous ruined sites in the northern Syrian Limestone Massif. The positive memories of many years of work in Syria were overlaid by the shock of the drastic changes in the very places I was familiar with.

The publication of my last project was accompanied by the reports on the events in Syria. It was finished in 2015 and I was able to celebrate it together with the excavation team over a meal in my favourite Italian restaurant. I then began writing down negative and positive memories – for my son Julian and as a kind of therapy for myself. I attempted to understand: What were you experiencing in the decades before 2011? Which memories do you have of conversations and situations during the last excavation campaigns in al-Andarin?

I have not drawn on the many photos and drawings of my publications in the following reports. Although they are archived in an institute of my scientific discipline, I could have made a large selection. Yet I hope that these reports are illustrative despite the few photos that I have added in the style of notes. I do not quote the Arabic place names here in the transcription that predominates in French publications, and which I also adopted in my publications. In view of the bilingual nature of my reports, I have – *nolens volens* – chosen the citation method preferred in English publications. I wish to thank Claudia Badde for the english translation of the text.

Far too many of the staff and supporters who appear in the illustrations are no longer alive. They belong to the events and memories recounted here and that is why a few plates of individuals are added after the images of places and monuments – *in memoriam*.

I would like to thank my son Julian, Renate Marzolff and Achim Arbeiter, who convinced me that it made sense to publish these reports. It was only after the events in Qalʿat Simʿan that I realised that they could be a small contribution to forward-looking projects of SIMAT, 'Syrians for Heritage Association' and the 'Syrian Heritage Archive Projekt'.

I am grateful for the acceptance and support of my publication by Katrin Bemmann and her team. The necessary steps for a publishment as an e-book were overwhelming, and yet Fedor Schlimbach mastered them – to him I owe special thanks.

Heidelberg 14th February 2022.

Contents

Als Archäologin in Syrien 5

Preface 87
Contents 89
Introduction 91

The first project: Documentation in the North Syrian Limestone Massif 93
    1971. Departure for Syria 93
        The Founding of the Institut Français and the years after Syrian Independence 94
    1973. Reorganization of the Mission archéologique de Haute Syrie; *"retraite"* of Tchalenko 97
    1974. First campaign in the Limestone Massif 98
    1975. Start of the civil war; second campaign in the Limestone Massif 104
        Journey to Izmir 108
    1976. Stay in Rome. Evaluation of the campaigns 109
    1977. Third campaign in the Limestone Massif 110
        After an accident, transport to Hama prison 111
    1977. Return journey by ship from Beirut via Alexandria to Venice 113
    1978. End of the documentation in Qalʿat Simʿan 113
    1979. Fourth campaign: documentation in the Madrasa al-Hallawiya and in Qasr ibn Wardan .. 114
    1980. Follow-up work in the Limestone Massif; preparation of a Syria Exhibition 117
    1989–1990. Journey to the ruined sites of the massif, which now belong to Turkey 118
    2016–2019. On the situation in Qalʿat Simʿan after 2011 119
    2019. Publication of G. Tchalenko's restoration work at Qalʿat Simʿan by J. Tchalenko 120

The second project: Excavation work in al-Andarin, ancient Androna 123
    1996. Return to Syria; preparation for excavation 123
    1997. Trip to Syria in spring. Survey and geodetic measurements in summer 126
        The neighbouring village Sammakiya and the Sammakiya family 128
        Recruitment of local workers and hiring new antiquities guards 128

As an Archaeologist in Syria

    1998. First excavation campaign; drilling for groundwater 130

            Building the excavation house 131

    1998. First activities of the three excavation teams 133

    2000. Expansion of the activities of the three excavation teams 134

            Members of the German excavation team; contacts between the three teams 135

    1997–2007. Problems of the ruined site: Bedouin tents, thousands of sheep and car tracks 136

    2001. Car accident before start of excavation; attack in New York on 11th September 2001 137

    2002. Return of A. Sammakiya; cultivation of the lands surrounding Androna 137

    2003. Continuation of the excavation 140

    2004. Restoration work in Androna 142

    2005. Situation of the house excavation after the uncovering of a floor mosaic 143

    2006. Excavation of the kastron church; celebration of the 'Day of the Desert /Steppe' in spring ... 143

            Situation of the church in the courtyard of the kastron 144

    2007. Campaign for the processing of the finds 145

    2010. First campaign in the main church of Androna 145

    2016. Destruction in the kastron of Androna by the IS 146

    Considerations on the *'Syrians for Heritage Association'* and the *'Syrian Heritage Archive Projekt'* .. 148

Notes 151

Bibliography 157

Tafeln / Plates

Introduction

> *"There is a goddess of Memory, Mnemosyne; but none of Forgetting. Yet there should be, as they are twin sisters, twin powers, and walk on either side of us, disputing for sovereignty over us and who we are, all the way until death."* (Richard Holmes: A Meander through Memory and Forgetting)

I worked in northern Syria and in a region of central Syria for almost two decades. The results represent the main part of my life's work as an archaeologist. During the years 1997–2007, extensive excavation work took place in al-Andarin with various excavation teams. In 2018, my last publication on archaeological fieldwork in Syria reported on the destruction at al-Andarin by the Islamic State[1].

In 2016, I received reports about shell impacts in Qalʿat Simʿan that destroyed parts of the pilgrimage centre restored by Georges Tchalenko in 1936–1942, as well as information about the catastrophic situation in numerous ruined sites in the northern Syrian Limestone Massif[2]. Even before 2014, the fighting in the old city of Aleppo had destroyed, through rockets and fire, the interior of the only still partially preserved Byzantine church of ancient Beroea, a space I had preserved with photos and drawings in 1979 together with the architect Heike Fastje[3].

How does one deal with such experiences?

In 1905, Gertrude Bell had made a journey to Aleppo via Homs and Hama, and on this route had passed through numerous settlements of the North Syrian Limestone Massif, which many years later became my area of research. I open the chapter on Hama in her report, craving for a glimpse into the time before the shattering destruction of recent years, and the first thing I see is a photo of the old city of Hama[4]. I had taken the same shot in 1980, before the devastation of the old city by the Syrian Air Force in 1982 (Pl. 1a). Ten years later I drove along the newly constructed asphalt road past the ruins of a few houses of the old city up to the luxurious Sham Hotel.

One year later, when I came to the North Syrian Limestone Massif for follow-up work, the situation had changed profoundly: Numerous small asphalt roads had been built as part of the Syrian government's tourism program. They now led to the ancient ruined sites and thereby facilitated the plundering of churches and houses for the removal of capitals and lintels with pickup trucks.

My negative experiences from the decades of the previous millennium were displaced by the destruction of Syria in the combats after 2011. But with the news and photos gradually reaching me, these in particular added to my questions about the sense of all my archaeological work in Syria and moreover to the significance of my older photos, drawings and documentation for future restorations and research in the region.

Below I describe the general situation that I encountered in the North Syrian Limestone Massif between 1971 and 1980 and in the Inner Syrian Desert Steppe north-east of Hama between 1997 and 2007. Should archaeological works become possible again there in the future, the situation in both regions will be profoundly different from the one I experienced. Since I have rarely addressed events and experiences beyond the field of work in my scientific publications, it now seems sensible to supplement these with a report about the overall situation I encountered in those two regions.

Only after completing both these reports will I look ahead to possible future work based on the most relevant results, and that is to say, to a situation that is completely open after the destruction of the infrastructure in all areas of Syria. My considerations about the purpose of photographs, drawings and documentation made many years ago will lead to the 'Syrian Heritage Archive Project'.

In my report on the years 1971–1980, I look back below at Gertrude Bell's journey through northern Syria, the recordings of the 'Princeton University Archaeological Expeditions to Syria' shortly before and shortly after 1900[5], the innovations in the French Mandate period and the developments in the decades after 1946 and before 1971. My experiences do not lead us to excavations of Near Eastern archaeology or centres of the Roman period (e.g. Kanawat, Palmyra), but to the Late Antique-Early Byzantine and Early Islamic periods.

The report on the years 1997–2007 will take us to a completely different situation: the excavations in al-Andarin of the central Syrian desert steppe. Al-Andarin, ancient Androna was the place I came to at the end of my works in the North Syrian Limestone Massif[6]. I had discussed possible excavation work in al-Andarin at the General Directorate in Damascus in 1980 already and finally organised an international cooperation there in 1996.

The first project: Documentation in the North Syrian Limestone Massif

1971. Departure for Syria

After studying Classical Archaeology and Ancient History for many years, I had taken up a second degree, inspired by a stay in Istanbul in 1965. These weeks in the former Byzantine capital had impressed me so deeply that I began to study Byzantine history and archaeology in Munich after my return: Instead of Central Europe as the 'navel of the world', the juxtaposition of Europe and the Near East had become decisive for me.

My first post-doctoral project was termed *"Use of Photogrammetry and Data Processing in the Documentation of Extensive Architectural Inventories"* and was funded by the Stiftung zur Förderung der Wissenschaften in Bayern for one year. Its focus was the North Syrian Limestone Massif with its exceptionally well-preserved buildings of the 1st to 7th centuries AD.

The first photographs of buildings in the Limestone Massif were part of the publication of numerous buildings of northern and southern Syria after the expeditions of Princeton University, led by Howard Crosby Butler[7]. The next major stage in the exploration of the Limestone Massif was the three-volume publication by Georges Tchalenko: *"Villages antiques de la Syrie du Nord"* – an exemplary appraisal of all aspects of this rich cultural landscape[8].

In 1971 I contacted Georges Tchalenko, the director of the 'Mission Archéologique de Haute Syrie', presented my project and was invited, together with Alexander Wetzig, a student of architecture, to participate in a follow-up campaign in 46 settlements of the Limestone Massif. The plan was to improve and expand the photo documentation for Tchalenko's second major publication: *"Églises syriennes à bêma"* [9].

The prodigious experiences of this trip to all regions of the mountain massif made a big impact on me. The number of preserved churches, houses, tombs was overwhelming (Pl. 5. 7a. b) and considerably more extensive than the publications had led me to expect. I realized that the application of any method of data processing should be preceded by an exemplary overall inventory of at least one settlement. I therefore submitted the findings for a description system in German, English and French to the foundation and began planning the comprehensive survey of a settlement with Georges Tchalenko, under his direction and connected to the Institut Français. He had already prepared a topographical general plan for three settlements with floor plans of the individual buildings. For one of the sites, all tangible buildings on the ground were to be surveyed using photogrammetry, complemented by partial excavations, and documented with analytical descriptions in a general representation.

When it however became apparent in 1972, that the planned comprehensive survey of a settlement would not be realized as a French-German collaboration and under the direction of George Tchalenko, I elaborated a project for the study of capital sculpture in the churches of the 4th to 6th centuries in the North Syrian Limestone Massif on the basis of the experiences gained in 1971.

In the 1970s there was no department of the Deutsches Archäologisches Institut in Syria. The Institut Français in Beirut was the centre for all on going as well as planned archaeological activities in Syria and Lebanon. It is necessary here for me to describe the situation I encountered in 1971 and to briefly discuss the political events before and after the foundation of the Institute.

The Founding of the Institut Français and the years after Syrian Independence

Calls for Syrian independence in the years following the end of World War I came to a temporary halt after the defeat of the Syrian army by French mandate troops at Maysalun, the exile of King Faysal and the violent suppression of the ensuing uprisings. The League of Nations recognized the French mandate over Syria and Lebanon in 1922. In 1929, Henri Seyrig was appointed Directeur Général des Antiquités de Syrie et du Liban. He interrupted his work in the Middle East during World War II with assignments in Mexico and America, before returning in 1945 for the founding of the Institut Français d'Archéologie de Beyrouth. In April 1946, the Syrian president declared Syria's independence.

The Institut Français was now legally subordinate to the Commission of Antiquities in Damascus, but all decisions on archaeological work in Syria continued to be coordinated with the Institut Français. It was Henri Seyrig, first director of the Service des Antiquités en Syrie et au Liban and then director of the Institut Français in Beirut (1945–1967), who with his all-embracing tolerance and foresight promoted archaeological missions of various nations over many years: the mission of the Belgians in Apamea, the British in Bosra, the Danes in Hama, the Germans in Tell Halaf. In 1934 he entrusted Georges Tchalenko, an emigrated Russian architect, with restoration work at Qalʿat Simʿān, Qalbloze, and numerous other sites in Syria.

The first project: Documentation in the North Syrian Limestone Massif

A detailed biography and an account of the years of his father's collaboration with Henri Seyrig was published in 2019 by George Tchalenko's son[10]. I will mention only a few dates from the biography, which preceded his arrival in Syria: Georges Tchalenko, after his emigration in 1922, had gone to study architecture at the Technische Hochschule in Braunschweig. After graduation he collaborated on some projects with Alexander Klein, Walter Gropius and Mies van der Rohe, and in 1931, against all odds, he became the head of the design office of the Technische Hochschule Braunschweig. In 1933 he left Germany. In Jerusalem he then accepted Harald Ingholt's offer to work as an architect on the Danish excavation in Hama. As part of this project, he met Henri Seyrig in 1934 (Pl. 37b).

I return to the planning of the recordings in the Limestone Massif. In their publications not only Howard Crosby Butler, but also Jean Lassus and Georges Tchalenko had reported about the intensive robbing especially of capitals in northern and central Syria[11]. Capitals could be easily removed from not too remote ruined sites, since they were accessible without excavation work (Pl. 7b). Because of their quality they were popular not only with private collectors and could be admired in Europe and also in America, in hotel reception halls or in gardens as table supports. After the impressions of the trip of 1971 with hundreds of capitals in the churches' debris, the research of such important evidence of the building decoration became urgently necessary.

The surveys in the mountain massif were to be preceded by the survey of Henri Pharaon's collection of capitals in Beirut. I had become acquainted with them in 1971 (Pl. 4). The 210 capitals of the collection were mainly from the Limestone Massif. In a letter to Henri Pharaon in 1973, I asked for permission to record the capitals of his collection. After his acceptance, I asked the Institut Français if Ernest Will would support an application to the Directorate General of Syrian Antiquities in Damascus for *"Untersuchungen zu den Kapitellen in den Kirchen des 4.–6. Jahrhunderts im Nordsyrischen Kalksteinmassiv"*.

After a positive response from both sides, I submitted the application for *"Studien zu den Kapitellen in den Kirchen des 4.–6. Jahrhunderts im Nordsyrischen Kalksteinmassiv"* to the Directorate General of Syrian Antiquities, which was approved surprisingly quickly. My following application for a postdoctoral fellowship at the Deutsche Forschungsgemeinschaft was approved in spring 1974. In April 1974 already, together with the photographer Helmut

Loose, I shipped the VW bus out to Beirut with Turkish Maritime Lines, began the project in Beirut and prepared the first campaign in the Limestone Massif.

All capitals of the Pharaon collection were measured and photographed by Helmut Loose with 6 × 6 cameras in the spring of 1974. The photographer and I resided in a very good atmosphere at the German Oriental Institute and were spoiled by Henri Pharaon: cooked for every day by several cooks – classical Arabic, classical European, Russian – under the supervision of his major domus. With Helga Seeden from the American University, Beirut, we went to Tyros, Byblos and the Druze villages of Lebanon, with Georges Tchalenko to Damascus and Resafa.

Shortly before completing my capital surveys, Henri Pharaon asked me to accompany him to one of the storerooms of the largest antiquities' dealer in Beirut: A dozen basalt capitals had arrived, a type of capital missing from his collection. Before transporting them to Europe or America, he wanted to select some for his collection. In the large warehouse I experienced a shock: a great many capitals and barrier slabs, entire lintels, large floor mosaics cut into small squares – they were all looted from Syria. After saying to Pharaon *"all basalt capitals are good"*, I turned around and left the hall. I did not suspect at the time that this shock was only the introduction to a long chain of experiences with antiquity theft in Syria.

For my surveys in the Limestone Massif these experiences with the large number of capitals in the collection and the confrontation with the excessive theft of antiquities in the warehouse at the port of Beirut were decisive: Some basalt capitals had to be bought quickly by Henri Pharaon to save them from being shipped to Europe. The work in the Pharaon collection was the best preparation for the surveys in the Limestone Massif. Collaborating with Helmut Loose, I was able to measure all the capitals and prepare short descriptions.

There had been a good atmosphere in the discussions with Ernest Will before my departure for Syria in 1974. My plans for the study of the capitals in the settlements of the mountain massif were favourably received, and my work schedule was not restricted in time nor in content. The lack of restrictions was perhaps due to the fact that Ernest Will, an outstanding classical archaeologist, was not aware of the exceedingly rich findings of building decoration in the Limestone Massif when I first began my work. The later problems with the Institut Français undoubtedly had to do with my broad formulation of the work plan.

At a meeting with Henri Seyrig in 1972, Georges Tchalenko had told him about my project plans. I was invited by Seyrig to visit him and therefore went to Neuchâtel in October 1972 to present my project to him. Henri Seyrig described in detail and critically how all the sites of the Limestone Massif had become French Concession territory as a result of the work of Georges Tchalenko (Pl. 37a). I noted that this Concession would have to be changed according to the opinion of Seyrig and Tchalenko, but did not see it as a problem at that time, since I had come to Syria and to the French Institute through the contact with Tchalenko.

Other topics of conversation in Neuchâtel were Georges Tchalenko's second major publication on the *"Églises syriennes à bêma"*, churches with a special liturgical institution, the bema. Before my trip to Neuchâtel, I had read the just-finished text in Tchalenko's flat and seen the drawings, most of which had already been inked, as well as the photos planned for the third volume. Henri Seyrig was expecting the book to be published soon in 1972.

When surveying the churches with this liturgical furnishing, Tchalenko had also considered the capitals of individual buildings. It was clear that my work in churches without bema on the one hand and the research of the capitals recorded by Tchalenko on the other hand would be closely connected with the publication of the bema churches.

1973. Reorganization of the Mission archéologique de Haute Syrie; *"retraite"* of Tchalenko

On 21st January 1973, Henri Seyrig died unexpectedly. Georges Tchalenko had lost not only a long-time friend, but also his most important sponsor. Even after his work at the Institut Français had come to an end, Seyrig had remained in constant contact with Tchalenko and had followed the work on the bema book chapter by chapter.

The difficulties that began immediately after the death of Henri Seyrig had already announced themselves in 1972 with the plans for a reorganization of the Mission Archéologique de Haute Syrie and had increased until the dismissal of Georges Tchalenko. In June 1975, he was informed in an official letter: His contract with the Institut Français would end on 1st October 1975; until then, his archives were to be transferred to the Institute; only after this transfer would he be paid his financial compensation after 40 years of work. Georges Tchalenko had had enough difficulties as a stateless person during the war and post-war period. Only in 1963 had his situation improved somewhat by obtaining Lebanese citizenship. However, he had not expected the removal of his archive, including his drawings and photographs for the book. His comment was: *"Il est normal, qu' on veuille se débarasser de moi à mon age, mais il est annormal, que l'on veut me couper la possibilité de continuer mon oeuvre, en me privant de mes archives"* (letter of 10th June 1975). Helga Seeden from the American University in Beirut commented by letter on the following situation: *"Nachdem alles auf einen großen Lastwagen verladen war, sah es in der Wohnung aus wie auf einem Schlachtfeld."*

Edgar Baccache, trained for many years by Tchalenko as a draftsman, was given other duties at the Institut Français: Tchalenko had thus lost his last collaborator. This was a disaster for the press-ready preparation of the original drawings of the book and unfortunately also for the planned monograph of the Church of Qalbloze.

It was not the civil war in Lebanon that demanded the reorganization of the Mission archéologique de Haute Syrie, because this had already been planned in 1972. However, there is no doubt that the death of Henri Seyrig in 1973 and the catastrophic events of the civil war had an impact on the thirteen years leading up to Tchalenko's death. I report these events because they also changed my situation after 1973.

1974. First campaign in the Limestone Massif

Before Helmut Loose's return flight in June 1974, I drove with him to Bashmishli, which was to become my starting point for the work in the massif during the summer. The trip with Abu Feisal (Achmed Abd el Ghafour), the antiquities guard of Djebel Barisha and al-Ala led to Qalbloze and Qirqbize (Pl. 3). An asphalt road up to Qalbloze was under construction. A boulder placed at the border of the street after the blastings came loose and hit the rear of the VW bus as it was leaving – a huge blow. The car skidded and with a great deal of luck I managed to avoid falling down into the valley. This was the first event that immediately reminded me of Gertrude Bell and her account of the more than difficult climb up to the Basilica before the road was built: it was all tripping and jumping over boulders, always in danger of tumbling down the slopes into the valley[12]. I had experienced my first climb in 1971 in exactly the same manner, and I nonetheless wondered whether the asphalt road really brought an improvement.

August 1974, I set out again for Bashmishli. Right next to the house of the guardian of antiquities Abu Feisal, Georges Tchalenko had built a small one-room building in which he lived during his work in the central regions. I was able to rent this house and it was my little paradise during all my work in 1974 and 1975 in Djebel Barisha and al-Ala. The wonderful hospitality of the family of the guardian of the antiquities, his help in the selection of workers and the organization of mules, as well as the thoroughly friendly atmosphere of the whole village, still shape my memories of the first years of my work in the Limestone Massif.

At this point I come back to the travel report of Gertrude Bell: She was on horseback and partly on foot in the mountain massif and set up the tents following the route. More important to her than anything else were the contacts with all levels of the Syrian population. Her superior knowledge of the Arabic language made any conversation about everyday issues as well as political topics possible. Unfortunately, my knowledge of Arabic was only sufficient for short conversations during family visits or official meetings and especially for conversations with the workers who accompanied me. I had a central place of residence in each region, from which the work in other sites was organized. Most importantly, my stays were determined by intensive work in one or two buildings of each site and only short introductions to the elders of each place immediately after the arrival of our small group.

Despite these differences, I was more than familiar with Gertrude Bell's report, as the situation in the limestone massif had changed only slightly by the time I went there. The ruined villages with their olive and fig trees, small tobacco and grain fields enchanted me, had become places of longing. Everything as crystal clear as if there were no dust at all, every notch in the bluish limestone as fresh as if it had been created only yesterday and ready to receive countless small blossoms (Pl. 5a. b).

At the first cock-crow I went out into the olive grove, where with the toilet paper roll under my arm and a plastic bottle of water I visited the tree assigned to me as my morning toilet – my intestines needed some time to get used to this rite. After breakfast of tea, crusty fresh flatbread, brined cheese, olives and yogurt, the mules were loaded: my photo cases, the large photo boxes, some tools, large bottles of water and the food for the workers, Abu Feisal and me. The hours before 8 a.m. were to be used for the walk to each of the ancient sites, because the heat set in already around 9 a.m.

My work in each church began with a plan that recorded the location of the individual capitals and other elements of the building decoration. Most of the capitals could be easily located in the ashlar limestone rubble, as they were not covered by earth or sand drifts. The workers were able to uncover the capitals, partially covered by ashlars, and shore them up with wooden beams to the extent that I could measure them and they could be moved for photographs. During the lunch break I prepared the work for the afternoon and tried to get an overview of the respective site and its buildings. The work could not as a rule be completed in one day, since its conclusion also included the reconstruction of the original find position of the capitals and a description of the doors and façade design of each church. Thus, the site of the previous day was often revisited on the way to the new site. The way back was always arduous with tired legs exhausted from going up and down the ashlar mountains.

The organization of Gertrude Bell's trip with tents and daily changing stations had largely corresponded to that of the Princeton Expedition team. I reached the individual places with my small team only after long walks – usually 10–15 and sometimes even 20–30 km round trip per day. But I also experienced the cultural landscape of the northern Syrian Limestone Massif without asphalt roads, on small mountain tracks and through inner plains (Pl. 5a). Nothing has changed the mountain massif as profoundly as the construction of numerous asphalt roads in the 80s of the 20th century – I'll come back to this later.

At the aforementioned meetings with the elders of a village, after exchanging pleasantries, I was able to have conversations about the family, possible illnesses and needed medicine. During all the stays after 1974, I then took as many aspirin tablets as possible, English fruit sweets in a tin, torches, sunglasses and small binoculars as desired guest gifts from Germany. In the company of the workers, my vocabulary increased from year to year. I was surprised because I was working with Kurds, Turkmen and Druze and I had a jumble of terms (including a surprising number of swear words) stuck in my brain.

The campaign in August and September led to a total of 28 locations in Djebel al-Ala and Djebel Simʿan (Pl. 2. 3), and once a week to Aleppo to buy mineral water, coffee beans for Umm Feisal, olives, cheese, etc. The campaign also in-

The first project: Documentation in the North Syrian Limestone Massif

cluded a visit to the village of Djebel al-Ala. When working in the individual places, I was able to build on the results of the *"Églises syriennes à bêma"*. This means that in the bema churches I supplemented Tchalenko's capital documentation and concentrated on the building decoration of the churches without bema and expanded it in my survey of individual house buildings. In many sites, two or three churches with highly contrasting capital and door forms had been preserved. The great differences between the individual church buildings raised the question early on as to whether they were due solely to contrasts within the workshops or to influences from the urban area.

Thus, in the always admired wide arcade basilica of Qalbloze – Georges Tchalenko's favourite building – I first encountered an extremely complex overall picture of the building decoration, which with its diverse forms of capitals, doors and cornices showed the coexistence of different groups of workmen[13]. The question was: Which craftsmen came from the mountain massif and which ones might have come from elsewhere, from one of the large cities, or had taken up forms developed there?

In September, I met Georges Tchalenko and Jean-Pierre Sodini with his architect Jean-Luc Biscop in Aleppo at the Hotel Baron: the documentation of Deḥes as an outstanding project of the Institut Francais was being prepared for 1975 and they were waiting for Georges Tate, i.e., to conclude his studies in France.

At the beginning of October I went to Qalʿat Simʿan and stayed there, after a short stopover in Damascus, until the end of November. I lived in the small house that Tchalenko had built in front of the northwest corner of the cross-shaped compound: a small wooden door led onto a long, covered terrace that opened into two rooms with simple furnishings. In this small house with a view down to the plain of Afrin and a wide view all the way to Turkey, I experienced the most beautiful time of my years in Syria.

At the beginning of October I went to Qalʿat Simʿan and stayed there, with a brief stopover in Damascus, until the end of November. I lived in the small house that Tchalenko had built in front of the northwest corner of the cruciform martyrion: a small wooden door led onto a long, covered terrace that opened into two rooms with simple furnishings[14]. I experienced the most beautiful time of my years in Syria in this small house with a view down to the plain of Afrin and a wide view all the way to Turkey.

After such a positive description, a comment is probably due regarding the frequently asked question: Didn't you have any problems as a European woman? In contrast to my experiences in Germany, I had no problems in Syria and it was Mustafa, the guard in Qalʿat Simʿan, whose explanation I am passing on here: *"You have a car, cameras, money to pay the workers: You are rich"*. And then followed a somewhat cautious description of my appearance (1.80 m tall), which rather reminded him of female figures from old sagas. What he meant by that remained unclear despite all the queries. Since Eva Strommenger had comparable positive experiences, her statement following some negative encounters in Germany is quoted here: *"I never had to suffer such discrimination as in my home country elsewhere. Especially in the context of my work in Iraq and Syria, my engagement was always recognised..."* [15].

My task in Qalʿat Simʿan was the detailed documentation of the capitals in the four basilicas of the cruciform building (Pl. 6). I was hospitably received and assisted by five workers wherever necessary. The elders in Deir Simʿan could still remember the years when they had worked on the restoration in Qalʿat Simʿan under Tchalenko. It was especially the family of the Kurdish mukhtar of Deir Simʿan, Beschir Abd el Kadr, in whose midst I spent many hours. They pampered me in every conceivable way: Early in the morning, a basket with olives, peppers, yoghurt, cheese, eggs, pomegranates from Dana and sometimes even honey would be placed at the entrance door to my little paradise.

At that time, only a few tourists made it to Qalʿat Simʿan. The steep path up to the east entrance was not yet asphalted, the restaurant in front of the north side had not yet been built and the place was not yet part of the excursion programmes of Syrian schools. When we came without a car, we walked the old pilgrimage path on the west side, up to the Plateau (Pl. 6a. 11a). What a difference to the turbulent situation I encountered in later decades.

In November, the winter storms set in. Mustafa, the guardian of Qalʿat Siman had strung a rope on the interior side of the south and west basilicas of the cruciform building, that is in front of the large openings through which the wind swept, along which I could safely reach my little house. How, for heaven's sake, had Simeon been able to hold himself high up on his column without roping himself – the interested reader should read the Syriac Vita.

The end of October was visitor time in my little palace: First Georges Tchalenko came for two days and for long talks about his work in the 1930s and 1940s in Qalʿat Simʿān. His report on the restoration of the entrance complex of the southern arm of the cruciform complex was particularly fascinating (Pl. 11b). Then the team from Eva Strommenger's excavation in Habuba Kabira came for a return visit – I had visited their excavation in September. They had bought all kinds of strange canned European dishes (wursti con krauti!) and several bottles of Liebfrauenmilch in Aleppo. Everything was lowered into the cistern at Simeon's Column for cooling (Pl. 14b) and later brought back up for a 5-star meal. Luckily everyone brought air mattresses.

During my initial documentations of the capitals in the four basilicas, I had realised that my analyses could only capture part of the multiple issues associated with the extraordinarily rich findings of the building's decoration. I had encountered some of the capital, door and cornice forms during my work in the three regions of the Limestone Massif. In some churches of the 6th century, however, the findings in individual forms led beyond Qalʿat Simʿan, and in a whole number of other buildings the overall picture differed fundamentally from that of the pilgrimage centre of Qalʿat Simʿan. My first impression was that in the broadly diversified findings of the sites of the Limestone Massif, I had in front of me a situation before and one after the construction of the Qalʿat Simʿan complex. That is why – despite the concentration on column and pillar capitals – the minimum descriptive survey of the overall picture of the building decoration in each individual structure became fundamentally important for me.

How was this great centre (Pl. 11a. 14b) judged in previous decades? Howard Crosby Butler stated in 1929: *"If we could but recover a few fragments of the Christian architecture of Antioch, we should probably find that the church of Saint Simeon was only a reflection of the architecture of the capital city"* [16]. Georges Tchalenko was the first to discuss the basic features of the building's decoration and saw a wealth of imported elements *"tant syriens qu'étrangers"* alongside local ones, first mentioning the involvement of local work groups[17]. All authors who, like Gertrude Bell, assumed that the architecture and building decoration were closely linked to the metropolis of Antioch, could not use any of Antioch's sacred buildings for comparison, since none of the hundreds of surviving churches had been preserved within the city or had come to light during excavations due to their deep submergence.

So there I was, sitting on the pedestal of the Column of Simeon (Pl. 14b), looking for a solution to a dilemma: I had found a way to go into the massif for a new project with the concession for the documentation of the capitals. Within a group of works or workshop, the elaboration of a capital was usually entrusted to the best-trained stonemasons. In the column capitals, therefore, rural traditions and any innovations leading beyond them are particularly tangible.

In the past months, however, I had come to understand that the capital findings should be considered as part of the overall impression of the building decoration of each individual building. Only this overall picture would make the character of individual groups of works / workshops tangible. Would I in the coming campaigns be in a position to record, at least by description, not only the capitals but also the findings of doors and cornices? And would I be able to include a selection of at least a few particularly significant pieces in my publication?

After completing the first campaign, I sent my report on all the activities of the first campaign from Qalʿat Simʿān to Afif Bachnassi, the Director General of the Syrian Antiquities Commission in Damascus, and applied for a second campaign in 1975.

On 27th November I regretfully said goodbye, drove to Beirut, took the car and myself onto the ship and drove to Venice. It didn't help that I had spent the night in Brixen on the 2. December before continuing on to Munich; after driving onto the Brenner motorway, an Italian lorry skidding on black ice wrecked my car on the 3rd December and I ended up not in Munich but in hospital in Innsbruck and in hospital in Munich another two weeks later.

1975. Start of the civil war; second campaign in the Limestone Massif

In the spring I worked on the material recordings of the first campaign in Munich, gradually recovering from the consequences of the accident. The paralysis of the left side of my face was slowly receding and so was the disorder of my balance. My broken toes were slowly healing, but a fracture of the temporal bone had severely and permanently damaged my right ear. The best news during my preparations for the summer was that the architect Alexander Wetzig, who had graduated in the meantime and who had already travelled with me in 1971, would take part in the planned campaign.

During the preparatory period, some of the events that led to the beginning of the civil war in Lebanon occurred: In retrospect, the attack on a church on 3rd April 1975 and the subsequent revenge by Christian militias who subsequently killed 27 occupants of a bus – most of them Palestinians – is seen as one of the incidents that triggered the beginning of the civil war in Lebanon. In the months of correspondence between Ernest Will, Georges Tchalenko and Klaus Wessel, who as head of the institute in Munich was in charge of my scholarship, there is no trace of these events, which profoundly changed the situation in Beirut and subsequently led to the abandonment of the Institut Français there and the transfer of the library to the Institut Français in Damascus.

The extensive correspondence was exclusively about the demand of a group in Paris to return all the photos that Tchalenko had given me after the trip with his collaborator Claude Vernet in 1971, as well as all the copies of drawings from his archive that were in my possession. I didn't want Claude Vernet's photos, because they were almost entirely unsatisfactory. On the other hand, I had already sent my approximately 3000 photos in 13 × 18 enlargements to Tchalenko in 1972. It was therefore a question of the drawings and photos for the bema book. It was no secret that I had already read the manuscript of the bema book in 1971 and received a copy of the text and some drawings in 1975. In my letters to Ernest Will in 1975, I had thanked him for allowing me to build on the results on the *"Églises syriennes"* in my first campaign and to concentrate on the building decoration of the churches without Bema. So why this reaction from Paris after two years?

It is sad to report the chain of depressing events in the last years of Georges Tchalenko's life. Some information has already been included in my obituary (1989) and in my review of the *"Églises syriennes à bêma"* (1992)[18]. But it is not until this report that I can describe how much my initial project planning and my subsequent work in the Limestone Massif were intertwined with the Mission archéologique de Haute Syrie and events in Lebanon and Syria.

One positive development should be mentioned that occurred during the second campaign: in 1975 Kassem Toueir became director of the Département de Recherches archéologiques at the Directorate General in Damascus. His extensive knowledge of the early Byzantine and early Islamic periods made him my most important advisor in the following years.

The campaign in 1975 focused on the settlements of Djebel Zawiye (Pl. 3). I had not visited the southern region, the Djebel Zawiye, in 1974, but had become acquainted with some of its places in passing during the journey of 1971. That first impression already revealed clear differences in the architecture of house and church buildings of the Apamene as well as their building decoration to the central and northern regions of the Limestone Massif, the Antiochene. At the very top of the agenda therefore, was a long stay in El Bara, the most important settlement of the region[19].

In El Bara, the house of the guardian of antiquities Abu Aboud became Alexander Wetzig's and my headquarters. It was located in the modern settlement that had been built opposite the ancient site (Pl. 7a). A very specific situation connected the two places: one family owned the grounds of each of the numerous churches. Low fieldstone walls enclosed each property and made every walk through the ancient settlement a tiring scramble over little walls.

After arriving on 1st September and organising a small group of workers, we set off for Deir Sambul the very next day. Rarely have I come across such brilliantly preserved, richly decorated houses in a ruined village. The sight of the church was also an experience: the east and west sides standing tall with brilliantly preserved column capitals featuring wind-blown acanthus in position of find (Pl. 7b). Both the high quality of the building decoration in Deir Sambul and the broken steel cable next to a capital whose cover plate had been deeply notched for removal, introduced us to the situation that awaited us in Djebel Zawiye: windblown capitals in churches as well as in houses. Among them, perfectly crafted capitals from the years before Qal'at Sim'an, but endangered by antiquities theft in places accessible by pickup truck. I realised that the larger number of house capitals of this type that I had encountered in the Pharaon collection came from Djebel Zawiye (Pl. 4b).

Unfortunately, right at the beginning of our work in El Bara, I have to address the situation in the guardhouse there, which did not make the place the *"magic city"* that Gertrude Bell had so enthusiastically described. We were on our way to Shinsharah, which had impressed me that deeply in 1971, when Abu Aboud's uncle (Pl. 37c) warned me: *"Don't be disappointed: all the capitals of the church are gone."* I arrived, saw the mess inside the church with the remains of what used to be nine capitals, and exploded. The workers, I was told, were impressed and very keen to work in the days that followed.

Abu Aboud had organised the removal of the capitals, and it did not take long to realise that antiquities theft was his speciality. Abu Feisal's attitude was completely different; he loved *"his sites"* in Bashmishli and suffered from the fact that he did not have a moped to make it easier for him to control the situation in his sites.

The first project: Documentation in the North Syrian Limestone Massif

We visited all the sites of Djebel Zawiye: Only Djerade and Ruweiha had a church with bema, which had been recorded in detail by Georges Tchalenko. The starting point for our work was therefore substantially different from that in Antiochene. For weeks, the focus was on the churches of El Bara, for which Tchalenko was the first to draw up ground plans and make partial photographs.

In each of the five main churches, almost all of them gallery churches, we were faced with a very special situation:

a) The centre of the church *extra muros* (El Hosn) had been cleared out for the installation of a field and all the preserved elements of the building made up high lateral mountains of rubble.

b) In the main church of the 5th century with the enormous collapsed layers of its two storeys, the capitals of the uppermost found layers had been robbed, deeply buried ones, on the other hand, had survived. The main doors of the west side, famous for the drawings of Melchior de Vogüé[20], had collapsed.

c) Despite the well-preserved eastern part, the features of the transept church had suffered the most: The interior had been largely emptied, fragments of doors and cornices had been blocked into the enclosing walls of the terrain, and some particularly elaborate capitals had been reused in houses in the modern settlement.

d) In the small church of the 6th century, the uppermost capitals had also disappeared, but it was still well preserved as a building.

It quickly became apparent that I had found and recorded some capitals of El Hosn in the Pharaon collection (Pl. 4a. b). This was repeated with two capitals of the Transept Church. In addition, the capitals of which Georges Tchalenko had given me photos to check had also disappeared. This left no doubt that documentation was urgently needed in every church. We worked with a particularly strong motivation, i.e. with the knowledge that we could not be sure of encountering the recorded capitals during our next campaign. We made find plans of the large churches, recorded some capitals in detail and the main dimensions of deeply buried ones, photographed the building elements that seemed to be important for the reconstruction of the overall picture and still had the feeling that everything was too little.

Following the documentation in El Bara, we drove to Apamea, the 'capital' of Apamene (Pl. 2. 3), where we unfortunately found only a few capitals leading back to Djebel Zawiye. Decades of antiquities theft had also affected the capitals here. Again, I was able to trace some capitals from the Pharaon collection back to Apamea. After relaxing days in the house of the Belgian excavation, fruitful discussions with our friends Jean and Janine Balty, who had been in charge of the excavation since 1965 and could only too well understand our problems working in the Limestone Massif, we left for Aleppo. The continuation of the documentation of the Antiochene sites was prepared.

The weeks in Abu Feisal's house, the overall harmonious atmosphere in Bashmishli – after the time in El Bara we enjoyed everything doubly. In the first days, Alexander Wetzig and I – supported by Abu Feisal and four workers – came to Bakirha, Dar Qita, Behyo and Bettir for supplementary documentation. Afterwards, the initial recordings began in Bankusa, Deir Seta, Kaukanaya, Djuwaniye, Meʿez and Bafetin. The focus of all the documentation was the capital sculpture of the 6th century churches, which, as in 1974, was expanded by recordings in individual house buildings. In this campaign, too, it became clear that supplementary documentation would be absolutely necessary in a further campaign.

After Alexander Wetzig's return flight, I went again in October to Qalʿat Simʿan and Deir Simʿan for a fortnight. During my final stay in Aleppo, I sent the report on my activities to Damascus to the Syrian Antiquities Commission, presented the results of the two campaigns at my meeting with the director of the museum in Aleppo, and informed him that I would apply to Damascus and the Institut Français for another campaign in 1977. I was grateful for the good atmosphere in the talks in Aleppo.

Journey to Izmir

The return journey by ship was planned from Beirut, but a phone call at Hotel Ramsis from the Deutsches Orientinsitut in Beirut on my last day in Aleppo changed everything: The situation in Beirut had worsened considerably – fierce fighting in the city, major problems at the port. I was advised to go back from Izmir with the Turkish Maritime Line. I immediately set off for the Syrian border and ended up at the Bab al-Hawa border station in a huge traffic jam of cars: it was census day in Turkey. I can no longer reconstruct what I said during my dramatic descriptions at the border and my calls to the governor in Iskenderun, but the miracle happened: I received the permit to continue and drove to Izmir with a large notice on the windscreen in glorious autumn weather on empty, car-free roads.

When I got there and parked my car in Atatürk Boulevard, I saw a bookshop directly opposite my car and entered. After choosing two books, I went to the checkout, looked at the elevated cover of the FAZ *"Beirut in Flammen"* and started reading. The FAZ sank down and smiling, the lady at the checkout asked me, *"Where are you from?"* I pointed to the title. With a loud shout, Harry Blackburn was asked to join the cashier and it was Elisabeth Blackburn – as I soon learned – who stated bluntly that I was to accompany her to her nearby flat for a warm bath and a good tea. I followed, soon enjoying a warm bath, the tea trolley rolled in, and I wondered how worn out I must have looked standing at the till. In the evening, friends of Harry and Elisabeth Blackburn were invited over, I had as much to tell them about Lebanon as possible, the souvenirs from my bus were unpacked and passed around. At the highlight of the evening, the Baron von Angeli and I discovered a passion we had in common: crafting necklaces out of beads and silver balls – what a day.

On the day of departure with the Turkish Maritime Line, everyone accompanied me to the port. I was standing on the deck and was tapped from behind: *"Turn around"*. It was the Pergamon Excavation team, who had also booked the last ship. On the way back, there was a lot of talk about Elisabeth Blackburn, who was known to all the staff of the German excavations. I gratefully enjoyed the little book by Enno Littmann about the story *"Vom Morgenländischen Floh"* that she had given me. For once, the journey to Munich after arriving in Venice was without accident.

1976. Stay in Rome. Evaluation of the campaigns

At the beginning of 1976 I went to the German archaeological Institut in Rome, whose library offered the best conditions for working out the documentation in Syria. I lived in the old town and enjoyed the relaxing and lively atmosphere in Rome for a whole year after exhausting work. In December I returned to Munich with the finished text and plate volume, submitted the work for habilitation at the university and applied to the Deutsche Forschungsgemeinschaft for continuation of the documentation in Syria. The proposal had been preceded by an exchange of letters with the Institut Français in Beirut and the Syrian Antiquities Commission in Damascus, who had given me the green light to continue the campaign.

1977. Third campaign in the Limestone Massif

After completing my habilitation in the summer of 1977 and receiving a material grant from the Deutsche Forschungsgemeinschaft, affiliated with the Institut für Byzantinistik in Munich, I began preparations for the third campaign in Syria. Better funding made it possible to employ the architect Ulrike Hess for the whole campaign and the additional employment of the architect Thomas Rhode (Pl. 37c) for three weeks. The documentation with 6 × 6 and 35 mm cameras as well as the surveying of the capitals and the documentation of the finds were to be in my charge, as in the previous campaigns, while the drawings of selected door and cornice forms were to be in the hands of the architects.

Again, Abu Feisal's house became our headquarters for a few weeks in August and September. We began with supplementary documentation in Qalbloze, Bettir and Behyo and then went on to detailed documentation in the 6th century churches of Kefr Kila, Barisha, Bafetin, Meʿez, Kaukanaya, Djuwaniye, Deir Seta, Bankusa, Bakirha and Dar Qita (Pl. 3). We had bleak experiences with antiquities theft only in the few places that were accessible by pickup truck.

The impressive settlement of Meʿez, situated on a plain, had already been hit hard before 1971: Of the rich capitals of the 6th century church, which Georges Tchalenko had recorded in the 1950s, only isolated small fragments were left on site. The capitals that were still present around 1900 in the magnificent church in the easily accessible village of Deir Seta, had disappeared, yet the overall picture could be reconstructed with some fragments. In the more difficult to reach Bankusa, the collapse of the interior was almost undisturbed, but in the great church of Bafetin, alarm bells rang at the sight of small splinters of a capital smashed in two for removal.

During the sporadic stays in Aleppo, we had moved to the Hotel Ramsis after the change of ownership at the Hotel Baron and not only saw the excavation team from Habuba Kabira again, but also met with compatriots from the GDR. I particularly remember their reports about the chicken farms and grain silos that had just been built in Syria. The GDR government's contacts with Damascus went back to the 1960s and also shaped the situation at the Directorate General of Antiquities and Museums: every now and then, a director general with a doctorate in Paris was followed by a director general with studies and a doctorate in West Berlin or the GDR.

In the last days of the fasting month of Ramadan, the two architects drove to Raqqa, Palmyra, Habuba Kabira and I alone by VW bus to Beirut. There were too many questions that could not be answered by mail or phone, and I urgently needed information about Georges Tchalenko's situation after his *"retraite"*. From the first day to the last, the days in Beirut were dismal and deeply stressful. After endless harassment at the Lebanese border station, I entered darkness on the Damascus-Aleppo motorway behind Homs – a situation we always avoided if possible.

After an accident, transport to Hama prison

Luckily, due to the strong gusts of wind between Homs and Hama, I was driving slowly when a tricycle without lights emerged from the ditch next to the highway and crashed into the front of my bus. The two farmers were sent flying back into the field, I extricated myself from the shards of the windscreen, tomatoes and potatoes and stood in a group of people that had appeared out of nowhere. The two drivers went to hospital and I to Hama prison. It turned out that, oh miracle, they only had minor abrasions and bruises and the young doctor at the hospital had prevented these injuries from turning into broken bones and other more serious injuries after their relatives' quick arrival.

I was delivered to the prison warden's room, who was celebrating the end of the fasting month with friends. Colonel Barakat was a French language teacher in civilian life and was happy to be able to discuss the accident with me in French. He went with me to the women's wing of the prison, where, as he had expected, I froze to a pillar of salt in the face of its dreadful conditions. Then followed the slight alteration of the duty room to accommodate the prisoner: a comfortable couch, a small tea table (a reminder of Izmir), the handing over of a very large key. It was the key of the huge gate to the Ottoman-era building, which would have opened the way under the nearby bridge over the Orontes in case I ever... since I couldn't go through the women's wing to the toilets in the men's wing... at night.

I fell asleep exhausted and with the enormous key on the little table next to me and woke up the next morning to the buzz of voices outside my door. I was visited with festive pastries: the night accident and especially the question, *"what on earth were you doing in Beirut?"* were discussed over and over again from the beginning. Unusually quickly, the accident was heard in court, I was sentenced to pay a not overly high sum of money to the two drivers, and after my architects arrived, I was able to drive to Aleppo with a temporary windscreen. Should the impression have now arisen that I magnetically attract accidents – the accident in Hama was not the last one I survived in Syria.

On 22nd September we went to El Bara, to Ruweiha, Mudjleya and Frikya for follow-up work and for the first time to the mosque in the neighbouring village of Kafr Ruma (Pl. 3). I will never forget the reception in the village's mukhtar: The women – unusually tall, slim, beautiful – welcomed me so happily and light-heartedly as I had never experienced in any settlement...

In El Bara, the atmosphere was as gloomy as on our last visit: In the main church from the 5th century, the large lintel of the west side had been turned over, and the decoration of the front, where the old coloured setting was exceptionally well preserved, had been exposed to the weather for months[21]. My letter to Damascus requesting that this extraordinary lintel be transported to the museum was unsuccessful. Excavation work by the Keeper of Antiquities had begun in the transept church and was all too visible. I could only point out to Abu Aboud that I would return next year, expecting to find all the capitals unaltered, and if not...

A great surprise were the reused capitals inside the mosque of Kafr Ruma: in it, the findings of some of the capitals of the transept church were repeated, revealing a 6th-century workshop that went decidedly beyond the capitals of Qalʿat Simʿan[22]. My photographs from the 1971 trip showed that related capitals were also in the courtyard of the mosque of Maʿarret en Noman and even led to the church in Qasr ibn Wardan, i.e. to a distant place in central Syria. The overall picture, which placed the wide arcade basilica of Ruweiha in clear contrast to the basilica of Qalbloze due to the lack of rich ornamentation in the interior, also led back once again to the journey of 1971, i.e., to the wide arcade basilica of Resafa.

It was thus clear that my next campaign would lead to sites in central Syria, to cities in the direct sphere of influence of the mountain massif – Hama, Idlib, Maʿarret en Noman (Pl. 2) – and above all to the only at least partially preserved 6th-century church in Aleppo, ancient Beroea. In my meeting with the director of the museum in Aleppo, I raised the opportunity for possible documentation in the Madrasa al-Hallawiya – the Madrasa connected with the former main church of Beroea –, and his response was positive. Following my work report to the Director General in Damascus, I submitted the request for capital photographs in the Madrasa al-Hallawiya.

After two weeks of work in Qalʿat Simʿan together with Ulrike Hess, I drove back to Beirut with her to meet Georges Tchalenko once again. Upon entering Beirut's Ashrafiye neighbourhood, I was deeply struck by the sight of the riddled and destroyed houses. I lost my bearings and, with the architect sitting next to me constantly berating me, somehow made it down to the riverside road. Indescribable was the drive through the centre to the German Oriental Institute, where we were greeted with the remark: *"It would probably have been better not to come"*. The city was divided into West and East Beirut. It was more than just reckless of me to drive the VW bus to the eastern part to pick up Georges Tchalenko, but… There we were sitting in the Orient Institute discussing the results of the campaign. Georges Tchalenko was happy to have Ulrike Hess' so delightfully good drawings in front of him and also relieved to be able to report on his catastrophic situation as well as the miserable state of the Bema book – everything was good and deeply depressing at the same time.

1977. Return journey by ship from Beirut via Alexandria to Venice

The return journey to Europe turned out to be more difficult than expected, because the Turkish Maritime Line ship had been hijacked by Mecca pilgrims. Henri Pharaon drove with us and his agent to the port of Beirut and negotiated. In the meantime, Ulrike had got into a dangerous situation: She took photo after photo of the people sitting in front of the cellar holes of their destroyed houses and in seconds was surrounded by an angry group of people. Without the agent's intervention, things would have ended badly. Then came the solution to our problems: Henri Pharaon had 'leased' a Danish ship at ample pay. We were loaded onto the VW bus and transported to Alexandria together with countless cockroaches. The return trip to Venice on an Adriatica ship was more luxurious than any trip I had experienced up to that point.

1978. End of the documentation in Qalʿat Simʿan.

In 1977 I had sent a copy of my habilitation thesis and a recently published article on Qalʿat Simʿan to Ernest Will, along with plans for the fourth campaign. In

1978 an exchange of letters began, which continued in 1979 and fundamentally changed my situation in the Limestone Massif. I had requested permission to make detailed documentation of some of the column capitals I had recorded in Qalʿat Simʿan, asked for permission to publish the drawings of approximately 12 doors and cornices, and considered it sensible to transport the endangered and particularly important capitals from Bafetin to a museum. The publication of the capitals of Qalʿat Simʿan was denied me with the reference to the imminent documentation of a French équipe: "*J. P. Sodini et moi-meme avions formé le projet d'une étude plus approfondie consacrée à Qalat Seman ... Cette étude peut commencer des cette année par des relevés consacrés au décor ornamental*" (letter from Ernest Will dated 26th February 1979). For my documentation of 12 doors, the Institut Français announced a comprehensive documentation of all (!) doors of the Limestone Massif in the near future; the transport of endangered capitals to the museum in Aleppo was not permitted.

What happened, however, was this: The 5th century capitals were included in the concession for my treatment of the 4th to 6th century capitals and were published by me in 1993 together with a small selection of doors and cornices (Pl. 16b). According to the last reports on the situation of the building complex after 2011, a large part of the column capitals had disappeared or been damaged, whereas the pillar capitals had largely been preserved. In 2016, the octagon and the entrance façade of the southern basilica of the cruciform complex were hit by air raids and shell impacts (Pl. 12b) – I will come back to this later.

The transport of endangered capitals to the museum in Aleppo many years ago by Georges Tchalenko had made a lot of sense, because it was the only way to preserve at least one capital of the church of Qasr ibn Wardan. The capitals of Bafetin, which we documented in detail in the fourth campaign, were taken away in the antiquities trade before 1990. I published them in 2002.

1979. Fourth campaign: documentation in the Madrasa al-Hallawiya and in Qasr ibn Wardan

In 1979, the first recordings took place outside the Limestone Massif, for I had obtained permission for the Madrasa al-Hallawiya and had been invited by Kamel Schehade to Qasr ibn Wardan for the documentation of the capitals.

The first project: Documentation in the North Syrian Limestone Massif

The permission for documentation in the Madrasa al-Hallawiya was a godsend (Pl. 8. 9), since none of the churches within the walls of Antioch are preserved or could be excavated. In the church next to the madrasa, which according to tradition was the main church of ancient Beroea, today's Aleppo, capitals have been preserved, which are of great importance for understanding the building decoration of the Limestone Massif (Pl. 9a. b). Photos of the capitals in older literature did not reveal anything significant, as all elements had been whitewashed[23].

Now all the capitals of the interior were documented and, most importantly, their whitewashed individual motifs were recorded in detailed sketches[24]. The result was fascinating, as I could trace the relationships of the capitals of a northern Syrian city to the findings in the Limestone Massif (Pl. 16b. c). When in 2014 the Hallewiyya al-Madrasa was badly damaged by shell impacts and subsequent fire during the fighting in the old city of Aleppo (Pl. 8b. 9c), the capitals of the western part, which we had recorded in detail, were hit particularly hard. Not for the first time, I was grateful that detailed documentation had taken place before the destruction or theft (Pl. 9a. b). I had brought two special ladders with me in the VW bus, which assisted Heike Fastje in the graphic documentation of some of the capitals and enabled me to make a detailed recording of each capital. The result was exciting: all the innovations going beyond Qalʿat Simʿan appeared as basic forms on the capitals and led to 6th-century capital and door forms. There was some evidence that these innovations were also known in the metropolis of Antioch, but the extent to which the image of the church of Beroea was transferable to the metropolis remained open.

With this new documentation, we went to El Bara, Bakirha and Bafetin for detailed surveying, as well as to the museums of Hama, Idlib, Maʿarret en Noman and Aleppo. In Bafetin, we were surprised by the sudden inspection visit of Ernest Will and Jean-Pierre Sodini in the 6th-century church. Heike Fastje was drawing one of the capitals and I wrote in my diary: What would have happened if I had just measured one of the unauthorised doors? I got up, told Heike that I was going to the church of Mshabbak for about an hour and disappeared.

During our stay in Qasr ibn Wardan, we encountered the already advanced excavations and restorations of Kamel Schehade and brought the two special ladders as a guest gift. We were able to supplement the previously known capitals with those that had just been unearthed[25]. We spent the night in one of the few mud-brick houses, which at that time were not yet part of a village extended by numerous domestic buildings.

The asphalt road to Qasr ibn Wardan had not been completed in 1979, and the tracks to places further inland were only somewhat manageable in Kamel Schehade's pickup truck. This is particularly memorable to me because it was then that I first came cross-country to al-Andarin, of which Kamel Schehade had told me miraculous things. It was reported in one of the churches there, that there were other capitals of the same kind as in the church of Qasr ibn Wardan. Shortly before sunset, after a gruelling drive in the pickup truck, we arrived at the southern church and in the last twilight I recorded some of these capitals – little did I know that eighteen years later I would begin excavation work in this very place.

This year, the outward and return journey no longer took us to Lebanon, but to Turkey: Venice-Izmir-Venice: the information we received from the German Oriental Institute in Beirut and from Georges Tchalenko indicated that the situation in Lebanon had deteriorated once again since 1977.

It was particularly sad to hear that Georges Tchalenko was not allowed to supervise the publication of the drawings of the *"Églises syriennes à bêma"*. They had been published in 1979 under the title *"Églises de villages"* and not with Tchalenko as author, but with the indication *"Dessins établis sous la direction de Georges Tchalenko par Edgar Baccache"*. This was an extremely problematic decision for the book, Edgar Baccache had not been involved in any of the documentation in the Limestone Massif and had spent years under Tchalenko's direction transcribing his pencil drawings into ink. It was clear that a publication without the author's say had been initiated with the modification of the title, the abolition of Tchalenko's intended division of drawings for the text volume and drawings for the plate volume, as well as the decision for the large format vehemently rejected by the author. As justification, the letters from Ernest Will and Georges Tate emphasised that Tchalenko only had an author's right for the text and not for the drawings and photos.

1980. Follow-up work in the Limestone Massif; preparation of a Syria Exhibition

When I came to Damascus in spring 1980 to prepare the Syria exhibition *"Land of Baal"*, the situation there been altered with the founding of the branch office of the Deutsches Archäologisches Institut in Berlin. There was now a contact point for all archaeologists working in Syria. My personal situation had also changed: I had been appointed to a professorship at the University of Heidelberg and would begin teaching there in the summer semester of 1980.

Together with Eva Strommenger's team[26], I prepared the selection of objects in the museum in Damascus and travelled to Mar Jakub Monastery near Qara, to Mar Aelian Monastery 10 km from Qaryatain and to Halawe on the Euphrates for the first time. The subsequent follow-up work in the Limestone massif concentrated on Qirqbize, Banakfur and Meʿez. This was the last time I was able to enjoy the hospitality of the house of the guardian of antiquities, Abu Feisal, because the French team had rented the Sermada school for the work in Deḥes.

I had hoped to meet Georges Tchalenko in Damascus, but only telephone contact was feasible. The events connected with the printing of the Bema book had intensified: after the publication of the first volume, the volume with Georges Tchalenko's photos appeared in 1980 under the name of Edgar Baccache, who had not taken any of the photos, in the large format that Tchalenko had always rejected. All queries were answered by pointing out that all the documentation Georges Tchalenko had produced, financed by the Institut Français, was the property of the Institute and that the author alone had the right to the text. Georges Tchalenko hoped to clarify the overall situation of the book in his Foreword to the text volume.

I had known the text volume since 1971 and – despite all Tchalenko's cautions not to tie the publication of my book to his book – I wanted to wait for the publication of his text volume. It appeared in 1990, only three years after his death and without the Foreword for which he had fought with the support of a lawyer.

The first volume of my works in the 1970s was published in 1993, after Alice Naccache's publication of *"all the doors"*, the second volume in 2002, i.e. after the start of excavation work in al-Andarin. The work by Jean Pierre Sodini on the building decoration of Qalʿat Simʿan, announced in 1979, is still awaited, but a few reports on their work have been published: The French Institute's work on the large centre had begun.

1989–1990. Journey to the ruined sites of the massif, which now belong to Turkey

During my campaigns in the Limestone Massif, I had often passed the Qasr el Banat monastery on the road to the Bab al-Hawa border station. Only once had I gone up to it for a few minutes, because it lies in the borderland between Turkey and Syria. In early 1989, I received a letter from the Syrian archaeologist Widad Khoury, who in the 1980s had begun work in the ancient settlements of Djebel Wastani, a region of the Limestone Massif that Georges Tchalenko had not included in his book on the *"Villages antiques"*.

Widad Khoury informed me that through her contacts in Antioch, now Antakya, she could get permission to visit the sites in the restricted military area. I was in the middle of preparing the printing of Volume I on building decoration and immediately decided to fly to Syria once again. We met in Idlib at the home of Souad, the headmistress of the primary school, and prepared the visit to El Bara as well as the trip to No Man's Land.

I first went to Bashmishli to see Abu Feisal's family again for the first time in ten years. Now the village had a water tower and there was even a television in Abu Feisal's house. A tourist now stayed in the small Tchalenko house from time to time, because tourists, I learned, came much more often now than before. Abu Feisal introduced me to his successor and asked me to drive him to Bshendlaya, where they had the best tobacco (Pl. 3). I went, i.e., first drove along the new asphalt road to Bakirha and Dar Qita. A minibus with tourists was parked in front of the Sergius Church. I parked my rented car and went inside the church. In each church, I encountered disturbed finds; the capitals I had recorded were either damaged or could no longer be found. I could readily imagine how easy it had become to park pickup trucks in front of the structures and load objects... I did not get out of the car on the way to Bshendlaya, did not visit any of the ancient sites accessible from Bashmishli. False sentimentality? No, this was a change I did not want to be visiting.

Even before our arrival in El Bara, we had learned at the museum in Idlib that Abu Aboud's son had wanted to sell a capital in Lattakia, was arrested there by the police and had to bring the capital back to El Bara. So after arriving, we asked directly for this capital. I stood in front of the capital with circulating arcades from the Transept Church, which I had assumed was 'secured' in its deep hole, covered by a pile of ashlars, after my documentation[27]. Abu Achmed's son succeeded his father as guardian of antiquities a few years later.

A final shock in El Bara was the reconstruction of the small church documented by Jean-Pascal Fourdrin[28], by a Syrian architect. He had managed to place everything incorrectly, not only inside, but also on the north façade. Had no one thought of copying him one of the old pictures of the façade? With Widad Khoury, I went once again to the places of Djebel Zawiye where I had worked. Our report on elements of building decoration – set up by the roadside, ready for removal – was received at the General Directorate in Damascus with some comments about the two ladies' trip.

I am still thoroughly grateful for such a different day in Qasr el Banat, Herbet Tezin and Qasr Iblisu, the places in the borderlands. Widad Khoury had received permission and, accompanied by Turkish military, we went up into the hard-to-reach places of Djebel Barisha. The magic of these deserted and unsettled places resonated with each of us. In high spirits, we returned to the Turkish military station and celebrated our farewell to the borderlands.

2016–2019. On the situation in Qalʿat Simʿan after 2011

When I received the first report on vandalism in the cross-shaped complex built around the Pillar of Simeon in 2014, I had no idea of the extent of the destruction to all the structures on the plateau between 2016 and 2019. The detailed reports by the team of the SIMAT – 'Syrians for Heritage Association' – not only about Qalʿat Simʿān, but also about numerous locations in the Limestone Massif – were more than merely shocking to me[29].

It is reported that as early as 2012 Qalʿat Simʿan was no longer controlled by the *"General Directorate of Antiquities and Museums (DGMA) or any other specialised authority that may be able to maintain the site and enforce its protection"*. In 2016, multiple bombardments, shells and rockets hit the entrance façade of the Southern Cross arm and the octagon of the building complex. An exploding missile not only hit the column and its pedestal, it also damaged the surrounding pillar positions with their archivolts. In addition, the mosaic floor of the 10th century in the Eastern Church was also looted.

The report's commentary on the completely empty interiors of the Arms of the Cross reads: *"The most alarming activity, however, was inside the church where the eastern and northern basilica floors are completely washed away, including the columns bases"* [30] – what a grotesque situation: after the collapse of the columns and after the restorations of Georges Tchalenko the capitals of the basilicas were placed in front of the interior walls or in the western part of the cruciform building. There I recorded them in the 1970s and published them – against all resistance – in 1993. Columns and capitals were no longer present in 2016 and, in a completely senseless action, the column bases had also been removed[31].

In the eastern basilica the decoration of the apse is not destroyed (Pl. 16a) and the capitals of the columns were published in 1993. With a capital of the eastern basilica (Pl. 16b), I look back to the capitals of the Madrasa al-Hallawiya (Pl. 9a. b) and to the capitals in the church of Deir Sambul (Pl. 9c): The void of the interior could be filled with a documentation of the old photos and drawings. The look towards Aleppo and to the south of the mountain massif illustrates the contact between the local workshops working at a high level and the workshops operating in the large cities[32].

In 2006, I had witnessed the excavation and removal of the column bases of the church in the courtyard of the kastron of Androna. I was told at the time that column bases were easy to sell because they could be reused in new buildings. I would never have believed it possible that something comparable would happen in Qalʿat Simʿan. Perhaps one day I will find out why the basilicas were completely cleared out…

It was only after reading the SIMAT reports that I was able to somewhat imagine how it had been possible to carry out looted excavations during the military conflicts in Qalʿat Simʿan: The reports on the situation in the ruined sites of the Limestone Massif demonstrate that all control over stone theft, antiquities theft, looted excavation was lost during the war years.

2019. Publication of G. Tchalenko's restoration work at Qalʿat Simʿan by J. Tchalenko

After I had received the text volume on the *"Églises Syriennes"* published in 1990, I remained in contact for over 30 years with John Tchalenko, who was administering his father's estate, and discussed with him the publication of the re-

The first project: Documentation in the North Syrian Limestone Massif

port on his father's restoration work in Qal'at Sim'an. As early as 1993, I had pointed out the important publication of the restorations[33], but John Tchalenko expected the French to prevent the publication and kept postponing it. It now appeared some 32 years after his father's death, with a superb biography and an overview of his most important publications.

The publication came at a time when it is doubtful that the restoration of the world heritage site can be carried out with just as well trained workers and with a comparably high standard of the architects.

Despite the long delay, the publication came at the right time: it will support the restoration of the Qal'at Sim'an World Heritage Site. I am not adapting my report to correct or expand on the current publication because it addresses events that were not dealt with in the publication. I am grateful to John Tchalenko to discover Tchalenko's preface to the text volume of the *"Églises Syriennes à bêma"* in the book, for which he had fought in vain for years with his lawyer[34]. I am no longer the only person for whom Georges Tchalenko's last major publication is inextricably linked to the events of 1972–1987.

In my work in the Limestone Massif I had followed the example of Howard Crosby Butler and his colleagues, albeit on a much smaller scale: As far as my strength and equipment allowed, I recorded a certain group of objects in about 60 ruin sites that could be accessed in the surface findings. There was, however, one major difference: The Limestone Massif had become French concession territory. The granting of concessions will probably be different in the future, because the ruin sites of the North Syrian Limestone Massif have become Unesco World Heritage Sites. Despite all the difficulties described above, the enormous problems of restoration will be in the focus of attention in the years to come. I will present some thoughts on how to deal with the documentation of Syrian cultural property made before 2011 after the description of my second project.

The second project: Excavation work in al-Andarin, ancient Androna

Al-Andarin, the ancient Androna, is one of the largest ruined sites in the central Syrian desert/ steppe (Pl. 2.17). With its two enclosing walls, ten churches, two bath complexes, a large kastron (*castrum*) and numerous house structures, it covers an area of 155 hectares. In 1997, excavation work began in al-Andarin / Androna as a collaboration between a Syrian, a British and a German team.

Three years after the publication about the excavation work of the German team in October 2015[35], the journalist Karin Leukefeld, accompanied by Syrian military, went to al-Andarin / Androna. She sent me the photos of the destruction of nine campaigns worth of excavation work by the Islamic State. The photos of the ruins of the excavation house and the mountains of rubble of the main rooms of the Kastron blown up with dynamite now hang on the wall in front of my computer next to the older photos.

The west gate and the high rooms on the west side of the Kastron, which we had restored in 2004 (Pl. 27. 29. 30b), were at the centre of destruction. However, it was not the remnants of the apse arch of the main church, the landmark of Androna[36], which stood about ten metres high, but the parts of the kastron that had been preserved up to a height of six metres, which were blown up. During her second visit to Androna, Karin Leukefeld discovered that the gate on the south side of the Kastron had not been destroyed.

In spring 2006 'The day of the Desert / Steppe' was celebrated in Androna. The mayor of Hama published a brochure for the festival guests, the photos of which show exactly the parts of the Kastron that were destroyed in 2016. The question arose whether there might be a connection between the 2006 event and the 2016 activities.

1996. Return to Syria; preparation for excavation

In the years after 1980, when the director general of the Syrian Directorate of Antiquities Ali Abu Assaf and the former director of the Archaeological Institute in Damascus Michael Meineke inquired whether there were still plans for an excavation in al-Andarin, my personal situation had changed profoundly compared to the 1970s. In my answer I did not speak of these changes, but referred to the fact that the publication of my work in the Limestone Massif was still blocked. Despite my best knowledge of how problematic it would be to organize an excavation in a site of ruins without infrastructure, I kept the doors open and did not cancel. After the long-awaited publication of Volume 1 of my first project[37], my head slowly returned to Syria.

In 1996 I decided to fly to the Directorate of Antiquities in Damascus for preliminary talks. During the talks in Damascus not only excavation work in al-Andarin / Androna were discussed. Considerably older, the excavation management in a 155-hectare ruined site was now problematic for me. I first presented my thoughts on a possible project in Qasr ibn Wardan: Survey and documentation of the excavated and restored buildings with a team of architects and excavation of the military camp located there. Unfortunately, the director general at the time, Sultan Muhesen, did not consider such a project worthwhile, as the site was already a tourist centre. The reaction to the planned excavation project in al-Andarin / Androna (henceforth always Androna), was positive. However, the start of the excavation was made dependent on the organisation of international cooperation, in which, according to the Director General, a French team should definitely be involved.

I could well imagine working with a team of British and a team of Syrian archaeologists. Cyril Mango told me, when I phoned him to enquire about possible collaborators in Androna, that his wife would be very happy to work with a team from Oxford and a meeting was immediately organised for the summer of 1997. I then contacted Abdalrassak Zaqzouq, the director of the museum in Hama. When he responded positively to my proposal for cooperation, I postponed all questions about the participation of a French team until the start of the excavation work.

After the talks in Damascus, I submitted an application for the excavation in Androna to the Thyssen Foundation and it was approved for three years. I enrolled Ulrike Hess, who had already worked on the Limestone Massif, as excavation architect. The geodetic documentation of the site was done by a team from the Technical University of Karlsruhe, the processing of the small finds was to be in the hands of Peter Knötzele and Marion Seibel, and Ina Eichner as well as the excavation technician Holger Hirth were recruited as close collaborators for the excavation sections.

The most important collaborator in organising the work before the excavation began was Ghassan al Shamat from Damascus, whom I had met there, at

The second project: Excavation work in al-Andarin, ancient Androna

the German Archaeological Institute. The following problems had to be solved before the excavation began:

- The accommodation of the excavation team in a house not too far away from Androna.

- The daily supply of drinking water and food for the team.

- The drilling for groundwater, which – even if it should be salty – was necessary for the toilets, kitchen work, etc.

- The recruitment of workers in the villages of the region and – ideally – also the hiring of a cook.

All these considerations were closely linked to the essentially problematic geographical location of the ruined site (Pl. 17). Like all places in Inner Syria, it was difficult to manage from Damascus or from Aleppo and Hama: The asphalt road to Aleppo was in miserable condition and the asphalt road to Androna's largest neighbouring villages – Homeh and Masluchiyye – had only been completed a few years before our project began. The region between al-Hamra and Masluchiyye was officially under the administration of Aleppo. But already after the first campaigns in Androna, all decisions were made in favour of the commissioner as the official government representative, as well as the hiring and payment of the guards at the ruins site from Damascus – albeit in consultation with the director of the museum and the mayor of Hama.

It quickly became apparent that only some of the problems could be solved before the first campaign began. So it was decided to start the geodetic documentation of the site and the documentation of all tangible findings on the surface with a small team.

The antiquities guard of Androna at the time, Abu Mamduch, had offered his house for rent because his family was living in tents. The house was ruinous: piles of empty arak bottles, broken windows and doors, defective power lines, filthy walls, the electric pump of the well had disappeared years ago and there was no toilet of any kind. So I went with Ghassan to Hama to buy the building materials for the house and the planned toilet house, the purchase of an electric pump and large supplies of drinking water, beer and all the necessities of life.

My first visit before starting the excavation was to the building complex of Qasr ibn Wardan, where I had not been since 1979 (Pl. 10). On the drive to Hama, I had already noted with appreciation that the asphalt road had been completed and now led beyond the neighbouring village of Androna to Masluchiye. The dirt road to Androna, which turns off from this road shortly after the village of Homeh, was so difficult to drive on, that the acquisition of an off-road vehicle was added to the list of absolute necessities.

After Ghassan had organised the team for the restoration of the house in Homeh and the construction of the toilet house, I went back to Damascus. I introduced the members of the German team and the plan for the planned work in Androna to the Antiquities Commission and flew back to Germany with the preliminary contract for an international team working in Androna.

1997. Trip to Syria in spring. Survey and geodetic measurements in summer

I was only too aware from the outset that looking after my son during the months of excavation would be a challenge to be solved every year. I therefore travelled with Julian to Syria in the spring of 1997 to show him the place where I would be staying for several months in the coming years. After a few days in Damascus, the journey led first to Qasr ibn Wardan and then to Androna. During the subsequent stay in Qalʿat Simʿan, we realised that the trip would be have to be continued at a later date. It was planned for the years after the completion of the excavation work...

On 14th August, I travelled by Range Rover to Venice and after arriving in Izmir, I then took the Turkish shipping line and drove via Konya to the Syrian border station Bab al-Hawa. Before starting work in Androna, I had to present the work plan for 1997 to the Antiquities Commission in Damascus and fill out the forms for the German team to collaborate with the English team. The Director General Sultan Muhesen promised to send a commissioner to Home and to support the cooperation of a Syrian team from Hama – meanwhile the question of the participation of a French team remained open.

With Ghassan I went first to Hama for preliminary talks with Abdalrassak Zaqzouq and then on to Qasr ibn Wardan to discuss with Abu Hussein (Sheikh Ali al Sharif) the question of the involvement of local workers.

The first campaign in Androna in the summer and autumn of 1997 was entirely devoted to geodetic documentation and the study of the surface features of the huge site. After Ghassan and I had picked up the two geodesists and the architect at Aleppo airport, the launch of the campaign was celebrated at the Ramsis

Hotel. Afterwards, we went shopping in the souk: The Range Rover was fully loaded with mattresses, bedding, pots, dishes and large supplies of tea, coffee, rice and drinking water. Since Ghassan had fortunately come with his own car, we were all able to drive to Homeh together afterwards.

Starting 18th September our small team with the newly arrived Syrian Commissioner Nissar Eleki was extended for a few weeks by Marlia Mundell Mango, the future leader of the British team, who was accompanied by her husband Cyril Mango. Although the daily routine was a bit tricky, as Ghassan had gone back to Damascus and we had to organise the journey to Androna and our stay with only one car, the atmosphere in September was good.

The work of the geodesists was accompanied by the detailed journal of Ulrike Hess with the precious documentation of the survey and her extensive recordings of individual objects. I explored the 155-hectare site kilometre-by-kilometre, recording tangible findings on the surface day after day until I was exhausted. It took me a few days to realise that the numerous round mounds of rubble we encountered in the central regions of Androna belonged to former 'Trulli' (Bienenkorbhäuser), i.e. were remnants of the post-settlement of the site. When, on the paths in the northern part of the village, I came across a church that was not yet known and encountered the raised features of the outer wall, that does not exist in Howard Crosby Butler's publication[38], I realised that all previous publications had only covered a small part of the large settlement (Pl. 18).

We had moved into the renovated house of the former guardian of antiquities in August 1997. Fortunately, the construction of the toilet house and the well with electric water pump had been completed before August, but the daily food and all necessities for the work in Androna had to be organised with daily trips to Hama and Aleppo.

We contacted the five Bedouin families in the village with invitations and gifts and informed them that we were looking for a cook and two workers to support the work in Androna. A month later a cook was found in the neighbouring village of Masluchiye, but no one in Homeh was willing to support the work in Androna in return for payment. In conclusion, it was probably this situation and the strenuous work in the ruined village that led to considerable tension between the two geodesists and the architect. Two young geodesists and an experienced female architect, almost twice their age, in a difficult situation that was extremely strenuous in a place without infrastructure. It was only after Ulrike Hess fell ill and left Androna in 2004 that Karsten Malige told me that the rift between him and the architect was so deep that since 1997 all work on the master plan of the settlement had only been discussed through intermediaries. Karsten Malige only returned to Androna in 2004 for further documentation on the town plan.

The neighbouring village Sammakiya and the Sammakiya family

During my kilometre-long walks through the ruined site, I met a member of the Sammakiya family in mid-August 1997, who not only gave me a copy of the map showing the extensive lands around Androna, but also addressed the history of the site in the first half of the 20th century with important information about this former property of his family.

When the ruined settlement was repopulated after about 1930, numerous beehive houses were built, especially in the centre, with intensive use of elements of the ancient buildings. In the late 1960s, Androna became state territory and all secondary structures were demolished – despite protests in surrounding villages. Numerous Bedouin tribes subsequently did not recognise that Androna could no longer be used privately, and we had problems with the 'use' of the ruined site throughout the excavation period.

Much of the Sammakiya family's wide-ranging land could no longer be used after the land reforms and some members of the family emigrated to Canada. The family's house in Sammakiya, the neighbouring village of Androna, was left vacant and a watchman tended the residential complex with the only tree we encountered in the Androna area in 1997.

I had no idea at the time that the return of the family, who had left for Canada in 2002, and the subsequent recultivation of their lands by Adnan Sammakiya would also have a profound effect on the situation of Androna.

Recruitment of local workers and hiring new antiquities guards

When I told Abu Hussein, the sheikh of Qasr ibn Wardan, about the problems in finding local labour, he advised recruiting workers in the settlement of Djenad, some 40 kilometres from el Homeh. They were better than the men from the villages around Androna – precious advice.

In the years to come, these workers, driven every day from Djenad to Androna by large pick-up truck, were extremely important for the success of the excavation work in the Kastron. Without these experienced men, we would not have managed the uncovering of the 5–6 m high excavation layers with thousands of basalt blocks and fired bricks.

Abu Hussein had thus not recommended men from his village or from neighbouring villages of Qasr ibn Wardan. I was able to reconstruct from his scarce information that he suggested hiring the men from Djenad as excavation workers because of the good experience Kamel Schehade had made with these workers in uncovering and reconstructing the buildings of Qasr ibn Wardan.

The atmosphere in Homeh was problematic: two of the five brothers who ruled the place with their families had surrendered to arak. A third was struggling to find tenants for his newly completed house. Marlia rented his house for the coming year and asked Ghassan, who had come to Androna again for a few days in September, to build a toilet house for her also.

The fourth brother, in whose house we stayed, was officially the antiquities guard of Androna.

We learned how he interpreted this task when we returned from shopping in Hama: He had taken advantage of our absence to secure ancient objects that he had looted in the course of his guardianship and buried next to a pillar in the courtyard of the Kastron. He was caught, sent to prison and hoped we would ransom him. Aid came from Abu Hussein, the Sheikh of Qasr ibn Wardan, whose influence in the region was great enough to secure his release without money (Pl. 10b).

Already in the first days of the survey of the surface findings, I had to realise that the finds in main buildings had changed profoundly compared to my first stay in 1979: Stunned, I stood in front of the deep looted excavation hole in the centre of the main church; in the south church, the central nave had been cleared out, the capitals I had recorded in 1979 had disappeared; in the Archangel Church, the rupture of a wire rope had prevented the looting of a lintel. Numerous plundered holes in the Kastron completed the picture. I had understood that the problem of looted excavations would also accompany us in Androna from the beginning.

In Hama I had to negotiate the hiring of not one but three antiquities guards, which means that each excavation team had to handle the payment and responsibility for one guard.

What was the situation at the end of the first campaign? The survey of the settlement had been completed in outline and the main buildings had been plotted with the tangible information on the surface. However, it was not clear when the geodetic survey work could be continued: The overall plan of Androna had to be supplemented by the numerous mounds, under which mainly house buildings were suspected. Thus it was mainly the aerial photographs with which I was able to give a first-hand impression of the dense settlement of the 155 hectares settlement during lectures in the following years (Pl. 19).

We had complemented the shopping in al-Hamra, the largest town in the region (Pl. 17), with what was on offer in the supermarket and in the Armenians shops. In Sroudj, Ghassan had made contact with Chalid al Taki with his large pick-up truck and thus solved the problem of daily transport for the workers for the coming year. The experience of the first few months had shown me that in future I should be in Syria around two weeks before the excavation team arrived to prepare for the campaign: I would stay in Qasr ibn Wardan or Sroudj and, together with Chalid and Ghassan, transport large quantities of drinking water and beer, sufficient coffee, sugar and tea, as well as cheese and jams from Hama to Androna.

At the end of the first campaign, I went to Damascus on 30th September together with Marlia and Cyril Mango, took my work report to the Antiquities Commission and then drove from Bab al-Hawa via Konya to Izmir. Before sailing to Venice, I called Julian as often as possible and was miserable about not being back until 12th October – too many days after his birthday on 5th October. In all later campaigns, I was able to organise the excavation work so that I was back in Heidelberg on 5th October.

1998. First excavation campaign; drilling for groundwater

The beginning of the first excavation campaign was organised differently than in 1997: The transport of the car by ship – this time it was a Landrover – was undertaken by two female employees of the excavation. I was able to fly to Damascus on 12th August, sign the work contract for the excavation at the Antiquities Commission and then drive with Ghassan via Hama and Qasr ibn Wardan to Homeh. On arrival at the rented house, we were in for an unpleasant surprise: The expensive electric pump had been removed by Abu Mamduch and sold. The wretched condition of the house we had restored pointed to the tent of the guardian's family, which was set up right next to the house.

When I went to the supermarket in Hama with Ghassan to buy a new pump and some groceries, I told Abdalrassak Zaqzouq, the future leader of the Syrian group in Androna, about the condition in which we had found the guardian's house and earned a big grin. After only a few minutes in the museum courtyard with a good coffee, I went back to his office and asked what regulations had to be observed when building an excavation house.

It became obvious that we would have to stay in Homeh in 1998 and organise the construction work from there. Already on our way back via Qasr ibn Wardan and Sroudj the preliminary talks and preparatory work for the construction of the house started: Abu Hussein gave the address of the man who would drill for water, an uncle of Chalid offered to manage the construction of the house with his work group, and in Qasr ibn Wardan Abu Hussein would contact the blacksmith for doors and windows. What remained was to decide on the place where a house could be built without any problems, to have Ulrike Hess draw up the construction plans and to organise the necessary funds. As we celebrated the quick decision with Ghassan on the terrace of the guardian's house with a few bottles of Almaza, a refreshing beer, everything still seemed unreal. First, we had to return to the present and prepare for the arrival of the excavation team.

Before the excavation work began, the specialist who had been brought in drilled for water. The water was only clear and no longer extremely salty at a depth of about 70 metres (Pl. 20a). From the very start, it was a treasure: of course, it was not drinking water, but it offered brief refreshment after dusty work and it allowed construction work to begin before the excavation work started.

Building the excavation house

Ulrike Hess had drawn the plans for the excavation house and on their basis the construction work was organised parallel to the excavation work (Pl. 20c. 21). Since Chalid from Sroudj was in charge of the delivery of cement and the production of cement blocks on behalf of the government, it was clear that the house had to be built with cement blocks (Pl. 20c). We soon buried our dream of building several 'Trulli' with mud bricks, as it was met with rejection from the beginning.

The purchase of a generator, which was urgently needed for all the work at the site, was unexpectedly difficult. We had been advised not to buy a product from China under any circumstances and after a long search we found a

5000 W-generator imported from Germany to Aleppo. At the end of September, the rough construction of the two toilet and shower rooms, the study and the kitchen was completed (Pl. 20c). The water for the showers and the kitchen was stored and heated in large water tanks on the roof. Thanks to a donation from the Chancellor of Heidelberg University, the initial construction work was paid for without any problems. All the subsequent construction work – the living quarters with their iron doors and metal grids for the windows, the large terrace with covering (Pl. 21a) as well as the furnishing of the storage rooms – I then somehow managed over a period of four years, despite all the refusals of my applications for support (Pl. 21b).

The English team had rented a house in Homeh for all campaigns and did not want to participate in the construction of the house by building their own living quarters. However, they paid for the costs of two rooms in the excavation house for the storage of their tools and excavation finds.

Already in the first excavation campaign, we were lucky to recruit a cook, Umm Saleh, from Sammakiya, two kilometres away, who was the good soul of our team in all subsequent campaigns (Pl. 39a). The most important provisions could be purchased daily in the neighbouring villages; potatoes, rice, tomatoes, peppers, eggs, olives, garlic and onions. While the boxes of beer and drinking water as well as butter, milk, different kinds of cheese and jams were bought once a week in Hama and the perishables were stored in the cooling boxes brought from Germany.

The cook who had supported us in 1997 during the difficult first campaign had, as a former dependent agricultural worker and under pressure from the family of the former guardian of the antiquities, been forced to deliver the money she had earned to them. The son of the guard – who I had just hired as an excavation worker – told us with a proudly swollen chest that he had paid a dancer in Hama for a whole night with the money. The fact that he was immediately banned from entering the excavation site for all campaigns was only the beginning of a development that had set in after the land reform in the years 1963–1966: the tensions between the individual villages – there were no common groups for breakfast and work – characterised every excavation campaign.

The relationship between the large Bedouin families and the formerly dependent small tenants played an important role in the organisation of the excavation workers. Tensions were particularly pronounced between the men from Djenad who were employed in the uncovering of the kastron and the members of the Bedouin families from Sammakiya and Homeh, who worked for the German team in the uncovering of the large house complex and in works around the outer wall. In the British and Syrian teams, a group from Sammakiya joined workers from Qasr ibn Wardan, Sroudj and Tufaha (Pl. 40a).

Out of this conflict-ridden situation, the experience with the excavation workers from Djenad stands out as a positive: In the Baath Party's land reforms (1963–1966 and 1966–1970)[39], they had received a piece of land. As poor but independent small farmers, they were so experienced in handling basalt stones and layers of earth in the excavation layers of the kastron that it can be said without exaggeration: they were the most important workers in the excavations in the kastron.

Even before the excavation work began, I encountered a situation I had not expected: at the beginning of September, large black limousines arrived from Saudi Arabia with refrigerators, stereos, etc., which were delivered to the Bedouin families and paraded from house to house for days. We learned that each Bedouin family was not only supported with 'luxury goods' but also with several thousand dollars every year. I could not imagine a greater contrast than that between the villages in the North Syrian Limestone Massif and the villages of the Androna region.

1998. First activities of the three excavation teams

I have presented the focus of the three excavation teams in the excavation publication and will only briefly discuss the projects of the first campaigns here: The British team excavated the 6th-century bath complex (Pl. 23a), with the investigation of the cistern in front of the south side of Androna, began the preliminary work for the extensive investigations into the water system of the entire region[40].

The Syrian team unearthed the structure to the west of the bath, which was puzzling in terms of its function (Pl. 23b). It was already clear after the first campaign that it was a second bath complex, and after the discovery of an inscription this result led to the Omayyad period in Androna[41]. The works were started by Abdalrassak Zaqzouq, the director of the Hama Museum, and continued in 2000 by his successor Radi Ukhdeh.

The German team began with the uncovering of individual sections of the Kastron (Pl. 26), the enormous complex in the centre of Androna[42]. All sides of rooms of the kastron were covered by a layer of earth; only on the west side had the lintel of the west gate remained visible over the centuries (Pl. 22a).

2000. Expansion of the activities of the three excavation teams

After expiration of the financial support by the Thyssen Foundation, I submitted an application to the German Research Foundation (DFG) for funding of the excavation work for six more years. After the application was approved in 2000, the excavation activities were expanded: preparations were made for the excavation of a house complex in the northern part and of two gateways of the outer wall – one in the northern and the other in the southern part of the site (Pl. 18). The official commissioners of the first campaigns were Nissar Eleki, Whafa Zaqqour and Waʿal al Haffian (Pl. 38b). Before the expansion of the activities, together with Marlia Mango, I had asked Bernard Bavant if he, as the leader of a French team, would be interested in working in Androna – unfortunately, he was tied to his work in the Limestone Massif.

At the same time, the work programme of the British team changed: After the excavation of the bath complex and the investigation of the cistern in front of the southern side of Androna, the extensive survey of numerous sites in the region began.

The Syrian team completed work on the Omayyad bath complex in 2001 and began excavation of a house dated to AD 582[43].

The work situation of the three teams was extremely different. The early Byzantine bath complex (Pl. 23a), which had been almost completely removed and was only slightly more than one meter high, as well as the Omayyad bath complex (Pl. 23b), which had been preserved at a low level, stood opposite the rooms of the double-stored kastron, which were up to 6 metres high (Pl. 31a. b). Later it became apparent that the rooms of the house complex were also higher than the two bath complexes (Pl. 24. 25).

These different situations led to the Damascus order for the restoration of the exposed rooms of the kastron and the house complex in 2004 – I will come back to this later.

In the preceding, the tensions between the local workers from the neighbouring villages of Androna were mentioned. In all the excavation campaigns, these problems were not transferred on to the members of the German excavation team. The contacts with the local workers and their families were not just good, they were the prerequisite for the success of the individual campaigns. I emphasise this because in Androna I learned to separate the antiquity theft by some local workers from the overall experience with all local workers.

Members of the German excavation team; contacts between the three teams

With the extension of the activities of the German team after the first three excavation campaigns, the team members changed. Holger Hirth and Ina Eichner (Pl. 38b) led the first campaigns of excavation work in the kastron. Ulrike Hess (Pl. 41a) worked closely with them and produced the overall plan of the kastron (Pl. 26), supplementing her documentation from 1997. Peter Knötzele and Marion Seibel were in charge of the pottery and small finds until 2001 (Pl. 38b) before Güler Ateş took over in 2003 (Pl. 40).

The direction of the house excavation by Ina Eichner passed to Fedor Schlimbach after 2004 (Pl. 42). During these years of expansion of the excavation work to widely dispersed areas of Androna, Christian Ewert was in charge the documentation of the soundings on the inner wall ring, the basalt circuit-wall (Pl. 40b). The documentation of the gateways of the outer circuit-wall (Pl. 26) was undertaken under changing direction between 2003 and 2006[44].

When the restoration work began in 2004, Karsten Malige returned to Androna and began to complement the overall plan (Pl. 39b). The last extension of activities began in 2005 with the uncovering of the church in the courtyard of the kastron and its mapping and graphic documentation by Oliver Hofmeister (Pl. 41b)[45].

The contacts to the Syrian team were easy to organise at the outset, because I already knew Abdalrassak Zaqzouq from the years of my first project. In the campaigns following the uncovering of the bath complex, shared living at the excavation site would have been an improvement. But a second excavation house could not be realised. Official representatives came to Androna three times to discuss a power line from Homeh to the excavation site – without success. In the event of a new start in Androna, the basic problems associated with the construction of the house would have to be solved.

Following the expansion of the activities, interaction between the German and British teams was considerably reduced. Due to the size of the ruins, the excavation at Androna was divided into three widely spaced building complexes.

The British team left very early for their various survey sites. I was only able to travel to Homeh once a week to share information. The Arabist Robert Hoyland and the architect Richard Anderson were instrumental in the contacts between the two European teams (Pl. 35b). Joint restaurant visits and excursions to nearby ruins took place at larger intervals (Pl. 35c). Only at the end of each campaign did all three groups meet at the farewell party in our excavation house.

1997–2007. Problems of the ruined site: Bedouin tents, thousands of sheep and car tracks

I already mentioned in the introduction that the Bedouin tribes did not acknowledge that Androna could no longer be used for private purposes. Our struggle against hundreds of sheep in the ruins in spring, the use of individual rooms in the ruins for sheep shearing, the erection of tents for large families in spring and, especially, against the transit traffic of cars through the ruins was only successful for a short time. It was Abdalrassak Zaqzouq, who had enough experience with the post-settlement of the ruined site, who supported us. But after he resigned from leading the excavation after only one year, I was left to negotiate with individual Bedouins – with a very different result.

We were thus forced to block access to uncovered rooms with stones as best we could at the close of the excavation. Even the western outer wall of the kastron was only uncovered to its full height in the last two campaigns in order to record the overall impression of the building in photographs (Pl. 22b). None of the three guards protected the site after the excavation was finished – the rich sheep farmers determined the rules. In the event of a possible continuation of the excavation work in Androna, the housing situation of the guards would have to be improved at the outset so that they could live at the excavation site after the end of the campaigns.

The fight against the constant car traffic through the site was hopeless and it remained futile because although some measures were discussed in the institutions in Hama, not a single one was realised.

The second project: Excavation work in al-Andarin, ancient Androna

2001. Car accident before start of excavation; attack in New York on 11th September 2001

I picked up the Landrover Defender, which had been transferred by two staff members, at the Bab al-Hawa border station at the beginning of August. We drove via Aleppo to Maslouchiye, a neighbouring village of Androna. A few kilometres before Androna, the right rear tyre burst and the car crashed down a slope, overturning twice. Luckily, the two students were not injured. Mudira was sitting at the wheel and was taken to hospital in Aleppo with multiple whiplash injuries and haematomas on her legs and arms. On the fourth day, Hussein from Qasr ibn Wardan came with a chauffeur – both dressed in dazzling white – and I was transported to Androna, lying comfortably in the van – wonderful.

When I arrived at the festively decorated excavation house with a neck brace and damaged legs, I was welcomed by a more youthful team: The excavation architect Ulrike Hess had brought two young architects from Munich to assist her (Pl. 41b) – great. Despite the enormous problems associated with the 'disposal' of the crashed car and my daily struggle in police stations, the mood on the dig was almost cheerful – we had survived and everyone was highly motivated.

This changed with the attack in New York on 11th September 2001. Victory celebrations were held in all the villages around Androna. As even my long-time co-worker Ghassan welcomed the victory celebrations, the whole team became acutely aware of the disconnect between us and all those with whom we were in daily contact. The events had an even more radical effect on the British team: Negative attitudes towards British and Americans were now no longer latent, but erupted openly. The Oxford team's excavation campaign was aborted.

2002. Return of A. Sammakiya; cultivation of the lands surrounding Androna

Due to the car accident, the excavation campaign of the German team was cancelled in the following year. Prior to our return to the campaign in summer 2003, the arrival of Adnan Sammakiya had changed the overall situation of Androna. In 2002, the boulder-strewn track leading to the site had been replaced by a fully developed asphalt road at his request. In front of the western entrance to the excavation site, the road turned off to the large house complex that Sammakiya had built in front of the northeastern side of Androna (Pl. 36a. b). In only one year, an administration house and several traditional houses had been built as living quarters. The luxurious interior of the residential wing and especially the large water basin in the inner courtyard of the building complex were not only a surprise, but also shocking: in the water-scarce region, an open pool whose owner invited us to swim (Pl. 36b): what was the function of this complex, built with a lot of money?

Adnan Sammakiya told me that he had emigrated to Canada after the Ba'ath Party land reforms (1963–1966 and 1966–1970), which largely affected the utilisation of his land. In the 1980s and 1990s, land ownership laws were further amended, state farms privatised and export and import regulations liberalised. Investors were intensively encouraged[46]. These were the economic and agricultural shifts when Adnan Sammakiya returned from Canada as a rich man.

Adnan Sammakiya's plans were far-reaching and focused on establishing plantations on the family's lands. For the drip irrigation of the plants, he had water dug up to a depth of about 700 m and was convinced that he had found underground streams – an account that did not convince me. In 1997 I had visited an estate (owner: Hasch Halul) that was irrigated with electric pumps from a 500 m deep well. So I thought it more likely that the precious, very deep and ancient water reservoirs of the region were tapped. I had seen too many villages in central Syria that had to be abandoned after excessive exploitation of the groundwater with electric pumps. Despite my scepticism, I keenly followed the progress of the planting of the lands, as this work had a direct impact on the situation in Androna.

The activities of Adnan Sammakiya involved the lands in front of the north and east side of Androna. A member of the Sammakiya family had already shown me in 1997, on a map showing the family's land holdings, that the estates to the north and east led right up to the walls of Androna. The British team had already uncovered the remains of a stylite column at the beginning of their survey[47]. It was only a few metres from the northern enclosure wall. How could the surroundings of Androna be protected?

In the summer of 2003, a year after he started planting, Adnan Sammakiya met with the mayor and the excavation team leaders at the Hama Museum. A contract was drawn up to ensure that the lands in front of the north and east sides of Androna would not be part of the agricultural activities. The contract was still not signed after 2007, but the lands to the east and north of the ruined site remained open at the distance stipulated in the contract. The British team was able to continue its survey.

The first negative news about the progress of the project reached me in early 2004: the large number of already set plants had, as was reported, been torn out by youths (?) from the villages in the region. They had to be re-purchased and replanted. The mood behind these actions and the essentially negative attitude in the region was also experienced by the German team during the 2004 campaign: The Sammakiya family invited the German team to dinner, but some members of my team did not want to go because workers from Sammakiya village had given negative accounts of the landowning family. What had happened? Adnan Sammakiya had provided our cook's youngest son with school bags etc. for primary school, but he refused to go. The cook's pay was judged too low and no workers from Sammakiya were hired to work on the land. We observed that the primary schools with the obligatory basketball hoops, which were built throughout Syria in the 1960s, were only too often visited by a small number of primary school pupils. And it was easy to imagine that the rejection of the family after whom the place was named Sammakiya had a long history. When I asked how much he paid for Umm Saleh's work, Adnan answered evasively: *"According to the usual rates"*.

But the destruction of the crops, while leading way back to the traditional struggle of the Bedouin tribes against the agricultural use of land, was closely linked to the negative consequences of the land reforms in the preceding decades.

Even before the start of the excavation at Androna, I was a frequent guest in the family of the sheikh of Qasr ibn Wardan (Pl. 10b), already mentioned several times. They lived in the mud-brick house of the Antiquities Commission, which was only a few steps away from the early Byzantine building complex. Abu Hussein remained my most important contact person in all excavation campaigns, although he was not a supporter of the work at Androna. Representing a tradition for which sheep rearing was paramount, he took charge of a few hundred sheep each year and was given a share of the profits after they were sold.

The situation of Chalid al Taki from Sroudj, our most important employee, was very different: The large pick-up truck with which he collected the workers from Djenad every day had been provided to him by the government and he had to pay for it over many years. He had taken over the transport of cement and the production of cement blocks. He built a large house for his family out of cement blocks, planted a small olive grove and vegetable patches, and held an important position in his village. For Abu Hussein and his eldest son Hussein (Pl. 41a), who specialised in hunting and training falcons, the bond with the government was a break from Bedouin tradition. Chalid was a role model for the youngest of the sheikh's sons, who envied his daily activities and income. Talking to Chalid, I learned that Abu Hussein's son unfortunately lacked the start-up capital for a small shop on the road. After consulting Abu Hussein, I decided to pay him this capital as an advance payment for future work on the excavation – this was a big mistake. The cost of building a small shop on the road was no more than a new room at the Androna excavation house. It was quickly completed, but it remained empty for the next few years because the money for the first goods was not raised.

As was to be expected, news of the whole affair had spread in no time and not only our cook expected an advance payment for her son's wedding, but also some workers saw an opportunity in such advance financing of their wages in Androna. I had made a mistake and could not really correct it in any of these cases.

2003. Continuation of the excavation

The next campaign did not take place until 2003: I had cancelled the campaign of 2002 to treat my accident injuries and finally had some time for teaching. When I came to Damascus in July 2003 to prepare for the excavation, I learned from the General Directorate that the requested continuation of the urgently required geophysical documentation had not been approved[48]. The second information came from the German Archaeological Institute in Damascus: for the television production *"Schliemanns Erben"* (*"Schliemann's Heirs"*), the documentation of the excavation in Androna was not only recommended, but strongly suggested. The third piece of information was important for all future work in Androna: not only in Damascus had the introduction and widespread use of mobile phones changed the street scene. The acquisition and use of mobile phones was so cheap that Ghassan immediately equipped me also, and he prepared me to be ready to meet all excavation workers with a mobile phone. Before travelling on to Androna, I was able to submit the re-planning of the excavation campaign to the Antiquities Commission. I came to Homeh on the asphalt road that led to the house of Adnan Sammakiya. My first thought was: if

The second project: Excavation work in al-Andarin, ancient Androna

only it had existed in 2001, when I suffered from every bump on the miserable slope with a neck brace and damaged legs. And the second thought led me back to the North Syrian Limestone Massif, where after the construction of many small asphalt roads as part of the tourism promotion programme, the theft of antiquities had increased. Pick-up trucks could now drive right up to the churches and load up whatever seemed to be good for sale. The rotten dirt track had made it difficult to get to Androna, whereas the asphalt road increased through-traffic and made it easier to transport interesting objects. I immediately drew up a list of all the objects that were to be brought to the museum in Hama at the end of each campaign.

The excavation work had just begun when the German Archaeological Institute (DAI) informed us that a television crew would be arriving at the ruins in a few days. Questions about the inclusion of the British and Syrian teams in the filming remained unanswered. I could only comfort myself with the fact that the British team was not interested in participating because they had started their survey outside Androna. The combination of excavation work with filming was somehow managed, despite all difficulties. We were preparing a lavish farewell party when a call from the Department of Antiquities summoned me to Damascus at an impossibly early hour. It was not only the harsh tone in which I was informed that restoration work would have to be carried out in Androna next year, but especially the ban on excavation work during the restoration.

After that depressing conversation at the General Directorate of Syrian Antiquities, I drove back to Androna completely exhausted and began to think of ways to circumvent the ban on excavations and to finance the restoration. During the farewell party with the film crew, I was not able to explain to my co-workers on the kastron, the house and the outer wall, how restoration could make sense at such an early stage, and what possibilities there were for financing, nor could I explain my gloomy mood to the director of filming – all possible solutions were still up in the air.

Only after arriving in Damascus at the end of the excavation campaign was I able to discuss with Karin Bartl, the director of the DAI, for which excavated rooms of the kastron, the house and the outer wall restoration might make sense at such an early stage, and what possibilities there were for funding. My application to the Foreign Office for support for the restoration was approved and I only had to work out a plan that would be accepted in Damascus.

2004. Restoration work in Androna

The restoration work in August 2004 focused on the west wing of the kastron: the west gate with the flanking towers and the high ramp house mainly constructed in basalt (Pl. 27a. b). For the rooms of the house complex built in mud bricks in connection with basalt elements (Pl. 25a) as well as the north gate of the outer wall, I had proposed as a provisional measure before detailed documentation, the structural consolidation of the mud brick walls with fired bricks from the kastron. A team from the Technical University of Potsdam was recruited for the complex restoration of the west gate (Pl. 39b), and the Antiquities Commission provided the largest crane available (Pl. 27). Abu Mohammed from Suweida was responsible for working of basalt ashlars that were used to restore the upper ashlar layers of the towers and the ramp house.

I was grateful for the support in all matters concerning the planning and execution of the restoration by Medjd Hjazi, staff member at the Museum of Hama, and Waʿal al Haffian, the commissioner on the excavation campaign in 2003 (Pl. 38b).

I had argued for the continuation of excavation work involving the uncovering of the vestibule that connects to the inner courtyard of the kastron (Pl. 25a), on the grounds of the 'sightseeing plan' for tourists desired by the Department of Antiquities. Fortunately, no official representative of the Department of Antiquities in Damascus was able to assess the extent of this excavation work, since no one had visited the site until 2004.

After the completion of the restoration works in the kastron and the house complex, new priorities were developed for the last two campaigns: In the kastron, the uncovering and overall recording of the church of the inner courtyard began (Pl. 32c). The investigation of the inner courtyard and the living quarters on the north side of the house was started. The second gate excavation of the outer wall was begun, and the overall plan of the settlement was supplemented by height surveys of the entire site of the ruins from 2004 onwards[49].

The reorientation was preceded by personnel changes in the excavation team, which represented a break in the overall course of the excavation project. When the old excavation team met again in spring 2007 for follow-up work at the excavation site, everyone was aware that the filming and above all the restoration work had such an impact on the overall programme that, in retrospect, the work of the years 1997–2001 represented the focal point.

The second project: Excavation work in al-Andarin, ancient Androna

2005. Situation of the house excavation after the uncovering of a floor mosaic

When a magnificent floor mosaic was revealed during the 2005 house excavation, it was immediately clear that it could not remain at the site (Pl. 25b). Through the museum in Hama, a team specialising in floor mosaics from Maʿarret en Nomʿan was called to Androna, and its transport to the museum in Hama was managed before the end of the campaign. Visitors came from the surrounding villages and even from Hama and Aleppo. For the first time at the excavation, I experienced local staff talking about a find: *"Such a mosaic costs a lot, the man was wealthy"*. In previous campaigns, I had not been able to convey that the buildings that were being uncovered, are part of their history.

After the appearance of the mosaic, alarm bells immediately rang in my mind. Interest in 'house excavations' would increase during the months of the excavation team's absence. The experience of looted excavations had left too deep an imprint on me. After the events in the years after 2011, I cannot however see a solution in transport to the museum in Hama: We know nothing about its condition after the looting of the museum.

2006. Excavation of the kastron church; celebration of the 'Day of the Desert /Steppe' in spring

When I came to Androna in July 2006 to prepare the excavation, I encountered numerous glass shards and fragments of chemical toilets in the centre of the village. These 'remains' and the tyre marks of cars and motorbikes on the house mounds were a great disappointment. The antiquities guards reported that in April the 'Day of the Desert/Steppe' had not taken place in Qasr ibn Wardan as usual, but in Androna. Twenty sheep donated by Adnan Sammakiya had been slaughtered for numerous invited guests who had gathered in their cars at the centre. None of these, the antiquities guards, had been invited, but they had cleaned up afterwards as best they could.

The mayor of Hama had published a booklet about Androna to celebrate the festival and they had saved a copy for me (Pl. 32). The local excavation workers gave me the booklet after they had demonstratively crumpled it up in front of me. It showed a view of Qasr ibn Wardan on the front page (Pl. 32a) and contained some colour photos of the west wing of the kastron. An introductory text by the mayor of Hama was followed by an English text by Marlia Mango and my German text. Only one of the colour photos (Pl. 32b) was astonishing: a montage showed the Syrian President Bashar al Assad sitting on an armchair in the opening of the west gate (Pl. 32b).

The remains of the desert festival and the tracks of the cars had a prior history. I had approached the museum director and the mayor of Hama in 2003 with the general plan of Androna, in which all the criss-crossing car tracks through the ruined town were marked, and asked for support in the battle against through-traffic. Numerous visitors of the desert festival had parked their cars in the centre of Androna instead of on the outside – the reaction to my request could not have been clearer.

The excavation team comments about the photo of the Syrian president were consistently negative at the time: *"The Western Gate does not deserve this"*. In 2006, I could not forget from the experiences in Hama: On the driveway to the luxury hotel built after the destruction of the old city, Abdelrassak Zaqzouq pointed out the ruins of the old townhouses to the right of the driveway, which – he told me – had been left standing on purpose. Every family I visited in Hama looked back with sadness – the events of 1982 had not yet been forgotten.

Situation of the church in the courtyard of the kastron

No excavation site in Androna was as unpopular with the workers from Djenad as the church in the courtyard of the kastron (Pl. 32c). In 2005, after clearing the rubble in the interior, we discovered that a dredger had so extensively destroyed the entire interior, that only a few centimetres of the original church floor remained. I was astonished that even the column bases had been dug up and removed. Had they planned to plant vegetables, potatoes or whatsoever inside? A worker explained to me: *"Column bases sell well. They are used in the construction of new houses."* So that mystery was also solved.

Adding to the bleak mood at the end of the campaign was the report from Nasser, the team's foreman from Djenad (Pl. 38a): The government subsidy for fertiliser and diesel fuel that was necessary to run the groundwater pumps, had been discontinued. Since many small farmers were dependent on electric pumps for their water supply, this decision had significantly worsened their economic situation. The problems were exacerbated by a drought brought about by low rainfall in the winter months.

After the end of the 2006 campaign, I spoke to the mayor about the desert festival and asked about the photomontage in his brochure. He spoke about Androna now being an important tourist destination following Qasr ibn Wardan, and his brochure was available in the museum for tourists. He did not answer my question about the photo.

2007. Campaign for the processing of the finds

In April 2007, members of the old excavation team met with the architect Oliver Hofmeister to work on the finds in Androna. An old VW Beetle was organised as a rental car (Pl. 33a b) – I could neither get into the car properly nor out again without problems.

The visit from Damascus contributed to the good atmosphere during this campaign: Abdal Rasssak Moaz, Director General of the Antiquities Commission, had brought plenty of time to visit the kastron and the early arabic bath complex. He stayed until the farewell meeting, which was celebrated with fresh mushrooms from the mud-brick hills of the house excavation (Pl. 34b), the rocket growing all over the place, white truffles from Aleppo (Pl. 34a) and beautiful spring flowers.

The information from Adnan Sammakiya in 2007 was also positive: the re-cultivation of the land had been completed. I was invited to participate in the first harvest, which was expected in about two years. I had been fascinated by Adnan's overall programme from the beginning – despite the unresolved water supply and the tensions it had caused in the neighbouring villages of Androna and even in my excavation team.

2010. First campaign in the main church of Androna

Under the direction of Fedor Schlimbach, the first campaign to explore the main church of Androna began in 2010. In the summer of 2011, news came from the Antiquities Commission that the antiquities guard of the German team had been dismissed for stealing stones. I suggested Mohammed, the son of Sheikh Ibrahim, as his successor. The representation of the German Archaeological Institute in Damascus, which wasn't yet closed at the time, transferred the money to pay the new guard. Thus, the guardian money was transferred until 2013, when it was discontinued, after the closure of the department and the altered situation of the banks in Syria.

The reason for the guard's dismissal was not surprising for me, based on my experience: he had *"transported away"* the large store of masonry stones, just over 9000 basalt stones, from the kastron excavations. I was aware that this stone theft had required several pick-up trucks and a larger group of workers, and that the operation did not only involve the guard.

Work in the main church could not continue after the first campaign[50].

2016. Destruction in the kastron of Androna by the IS

In summer 2018, journalist Karin Leukefeld visited Androna accompanied by Syrian military, and sent me photos of the destruction in Androna by the IS in 2016 (Pls. 28–31). She and her companion remained strictly in the centre of the village, as it was too dangerous to go round the whole site. The ruins of the excavation house were photographed only from a greater distance and the situation of the main church and the two baths were documented with a few photos. The deterioration of the excavation house was already well advanced in 2016 because the large iron doors and windows had been removed and sold in the years after a German excavation team's last campaign in 2010.

In 2015, the members of al Nusra and IS most likely did not live in the excavation house, but in the luxuriously furnished *trulli* in front of the north-east corner of Androna (Pl. 36a). Adnan Sammakiya had already left his residence and the lands before 2015, after the kidnapping of his youngest son and the release after payment of the ransom. In a telephone conversation with his eldest son in 2019, I learned that he does not know the condition the plantations are in.

All of Karin Leukefeld's documentation in 2018 and 2019 focused on the kastron. Even without knowledge of the ruined site and the activities of the excavation teams, it was immediately apparent that the destruction affected the west wing of the kastron. The gateway on the south side of the kastron was undamaged. An Arabic inscription on the tower in front of the south side of the west gate records that the 'Free Damascene' were responsible for the destruction.

The west gate (Pl. 29) and all elevated parts of the west entrance, the ramp house, the west hall (Pl. 30b), the latrine and the south hall (Pl. 31) were blown up with dynamite. Since they were built in a layered masonry of basalt blocks and burnt bricks, the dynamite charges probably had to be reapplied to each room. The partially preserved layers of basalt show that the destruction was concentrated on the entrance to the courtyard of the kastron, the entrance to the ramp house and the ramp ways to the upper storeys, the doors to the large halls and the high north wall of the south hall (Pl. 31a. b). The photo of a mound of rubble with the fragment of one of the basalt doors (Pl. 31c) shows that none of the doors – except the west door – can be restored.

The destruction of the main gate that had been restored in 2004, was not only a shock. It will continue to be painful until the gate is again restored. The lintel with the famous founder's inscription lies together with the inner lintel in the gateway. The facts, that the cross monograms on both lintels were not worked off, the second large gateway on the south side of the kastron was not blown up and the activities of the IS did not cover either the church in the inner courtyard of the kastron (Pl. 32c) or the main church of Androna, raise some questions. The lintel of the west gate had remained visible for hundreds of years even before the complete excavation of the gate, despite the approximately six-meter-high burial layers of the kastron (Pl. 22a). However, the real landmark of Androna was and remains to this day the vestige of the apsidal arch of the main church, which stands about ten meters high.

The questions led back to the brochure published by the mayor of Hama in 2006. The translation of the text written by the mayor in the brochure, which I had received[51], led to something I had not anticipated. The text describes the location and Byzantine origins of the site, cites the last mention of the site in 1225 by the geographer Yakut al-Hamawi[52] and links the great heritage of the desert to the glory of the wine of al-Andarin in the Moʿallaqat of Amr[53]. The final message for the 'Day of the Desert / Steppe' is: *"Today's rise of the Ummah (nation?), despite the harshness of the circumstances experienced by the Arabs, has not slowed down the progress and development of our nation. By following the footsteps of Bashar al-Assad, the President of the Syrian Arab Republic, we will become the role model of the nation that has established its ancient glory and will drive the building of its new civilisation. Once again, we welcome you to Hama".*

For the guests of the Desert Festival, the brochure was a well-intentioned welcome. My question about the image of Assad in the opening of the West Gate is nevertheless not clearly resolved. With the transfer of the Festival from Qasr ibn Wardan to Androna, the importance of the ruined site was recognised. But was the mayor aware of the possible reaction of the excavation staff to the whole operation? It is hard to imagine that members of the IS took the brochure from the museum. For members of the Islamic State, the blowing up of the Western Gate in Androna was one of many actions aimed at destroying as much of Syria's cultural heritage as possible. The idea that the action in Androna was somehow related to the brochure that circulated among the excavation workers is an unverifiable assumption.

Considerations on the *'Syrians for Heritage Association'* and the *'Syrian Heritage Archive Projekt'*

One of the motivations for my years of work in the North Syrian Limestone Massif was my experience with antiquities theft. I witnessed it over many years – accompanied by stone looting and illegal excavations – in all the ancient sites I worked at. The destruction in al-Andarin / Androna by the Islamic State in 2016 surpassed anything I had encountered before 2007 – the targeted destruction of the rich cultural heritage hit numerous ancient sites in Syria after 2011[54].

„*In truth, Syria has always suffered – and the regime always tolerated – a limited amount of theft from historical sites, to boost the economy in the poor areas in the north of the country and to enrich the regimes own mafiosi. But what is happening now is on an epic and terrifying scale*"[55].

The programme of the 'Syrians for heritage association', which was founded in January 2018 in Berlin, states: "*Through our cultural heritage we can comprehend our past and anticipate our future. It helps us to rediscover our plurality, restore our sense of belonging to our land and country, and achieve our hoped-for a peaceful future*".

The reports on the North Syrian Limestone Massif have shown that no civil institution exists that could stop the act of destruction. Likewise, it remains to be seen whether future improvements in the staffing of the antiquities services could at least partially curtail the perfectly organised and brutal antiquities theft – as well as intensive looting and stone theft. The problems of restoration are all too great and will be faced in time of peace by all those interested in Syria's cultural heritage.

The documentation of losses, the archiving of what still exists and what has been preserved in older photos and drawings has begun. In a major project at the University of Paris Nanterre, all older documentation on the Qalʿat Simʿan pilgrimage centre is being archived under the direction of archaeologist Micheline Kurdy[56]. The 'Syrian Heritage Archive Project' is dedicated to the numerous questions of digitisation and the transfer of the resulting databases within and outside Syria[57]. For the time being, the only possible contribution to the ongoing international work on creating comprehensive databases is that I have archived the materials of my projects in the institute of my department at the University of Göttingen and made them accessible.

Finally, I would like to return to the initial question about the meaning of approximately twenty years of activity in the North Syrian Limestone Massif and in one of the largest ruined sites in Central Syria. With the comprehensive documentation of photos and drawings of elements of the building decoration, it is possible to complement what is no longer available in many ruin sites. It is not about one or the other capital – oh, again a capital – but about a characteristic of the so-called 'Dead Cities': the outstanding skill of local workshops and craftsmen groups and their contact with the large Syrian cities in whose sphere of influence the mountain massif lies.

The situation is different in al-Andarin, the ancient Androna. There, the individual objects that were accessible on the surface had been so largely plundered that clarification of the history of the site could only be expected through the excavation of buildings buried under layers of earth and sand. The excavation work in the kastron and in the two bath complexes was not only rich in results for the early Byzantine period – the 4th to early 7th centuries – it also yielded far-reaching information on the subsequent use of the site in early Arab times in the early 7th and 8th centuries. In addition, the excellent work of the British team made it possible to reconstruct the ancient irrigation system and the foundations of economy and trade.

In my report, I have addressed the problems and necessary changes that would need to be resolved before any possible continuation of excavation work in Androna. However, it would be grotesque to present any further recommendations for resuming excavations in Androna – given the still desperate situation of the people in Syria.

Notes

1   Strube 2019, 67–75.

2   SIMAT, Documenting the Current Condition of Saint Simeon Castle Damages and Violations, Report 2017-2020.

3   A. Kilb, Trost aus Trümmern, FAZ 2016, 1-2; K. Leukefeld, Aleppo – die geschundene Stadt atmet noch, Neues Deutschland, 4. Mai 2017, 3.

4   Bell 1905 / 2015; R. Lefèvre, Ashes of Hama. The Muslim Brotherhood in Syria, London 2013.

5   Butler 1920, *passim*.

6   Strube 2015, I-II, *passim*.

7   Butler 1920, *passim*.

8   Tchalenko 1953, *passim*.

9   Tchalenko 1980-1990, *passim*.

10 Loosley Leeming – Tchalenko 2019, 1-26.

11 Butler 1920, 48 mentions illegal excavations. Tchalenko 1953, I, 16 mentions Tell Minnis, not far from Androna, as a centre for organized antiquities theft. Lassus' passage on the theft of antique capitals for new buildings is characteristic (Lassus 1935–36, I, 207).

12 Bell 1905 / 2015, 266.

13 Strube 1993, 94-115.

14 Loosley Leeming – Tchalenko 2019, fig. 1.19.

15 S. Böhme, Männer jagen, Frauen sammeln, Berlin – Tübingen 2012, 194.

16 Butler 1929, 98.

17 Tchalenko 1953 I, 233f.; Strube 1993, 270.

18 Ch. Strube, Georges Tchalenko, Églises syriennes à bêma, Jahrbuch für Antike und Christentum 35, 1992, 222-228; Ch. Strube: Nachruf Georges Tchalenko, Gnomon 60, 1988, 667-668.

19 Strube 1993, 143-197; Strube 2002, 157-164.

20 de Vogüé 1865–1877, Taf. 62.

21 Ch. Strube, Die „Toten Städte". Stadt und Land in Nordsyrien während der Spätantike, Zaberns Bildbände zur Archäologie, Mainz 1996, 48 Abb. 84.

22 Strube 1993, 65-68, Taf. 35a. b.

23 Strube 2002, 5-16.

24 Strube 2002, Abb. 1a-l. 2a-g.

25 Strube 2002, 61 ff. 79 ff. Taf. 51.

26 The exhibition „*Land des Baal, Syrien – Forum der Völker und Kulturen*" was organised by Eva Strommenger. It began 1982 at Berlin, in the Great Orangerie of 'Schloss Charlottenburg'.

27 Strube 2002, Taf. 22.

28 J.-P. Fourdrin, Église E.5 d'El Bara, Syria 69, 1992, 170-210.

29 SIMAT, Syrians for Heritage, Documenting the Current Condition of Saint Simeon Castle Damages and Violations, 2017-2020, 1-22. They generously allowed me to publish the photos of the destructions.

30 *ibid.* 11.

31 See Strube 2015, 198. 211-213. The situation in the church of the kastron of Androna is comparable: The interior of the church was completely robbed out and even the bases of the columns were excavated.

32 In detail Strube 1993, 209-217. 241-244. 267-270; Strube 2002, 215-225. See also the commentary of B. Bavant, Les églises du Massif Calcaire de Syrie du Nord (VIe–VIIe s.), Journal of Roman Archaeology 2, 2005, 756-770.

33 Strube 1993, 205 Anm. 1135.

34 Loosly Leeming – Tchalenko 2019, 26. The article of the co-author is more than only problematic and this not only because she has problems with german publications.

35 Strube 2015, I-II, *passim*.

36 Schlimbach 2020, Taf. 8a.

37 Strube 1993, *passim*.

38 Butler 1920, 8-10.

39 D. Zevenhuizen, Land, Conflict and Agriculture in Syria, Wageningen University, Wageningen 2016, 11-27.

40 Mango 2010, 245–290, 245-270.

41 Strube 2015, I, 273 und 291f.

42 Strube 2015, I, 87-194.

43 After two campaigns excavations were finished.

44 Strube 2015, I, 69-85.

45 Strube 2015, I, 192-220.

46 Zevenhuizen 2016 (see above note 39), 14-19.

47 Mango 2010, 245–290, 274 f. fig. 28. 38.

48 Strube 2015, I, 56-60; Abb. 15.

49 Strube 2015, II, Plan 3.

50 Schlimbach 2020.

51 I thank Liana Saif for the translation of the difficult text.

52 For Yakut al Halawi see Strube 2015, I, 7.

53 The verses of Amr ibn Kultum (died 584) celebrate the wine of Androna: „*Ha girl! Up with the bowl! Give us our dawn draught and do not spare the wines of Andarine*", see also Strube 2015, I, 7 f.

54 R. Fisk, Syria's ancient treasures pulverised, Independent, 5. August 2012, 1-4.

55 *ibid.* 3-4.

56 Micheline Kurdy, Numérisation et accès aux archives archéologiques du site de Saint-Syméon. The project is integrated in the ‚Fondation Aleph', the ‚Alliance internationale pour la protection du patrimoine dans les zones de conflits'.

57 Issam Ballouz, Die digitale Rettung des syrischen Kulturerbes: Grenzen und Chancen, Syrian Heritage Archive Projekt, 2017, 66-74.

Bibliography

Bell 1905: G. Bell, Am Ende des Lavastroms. Durch die Wüsten und Kulturstätten Syriens (1905). Ed. by G. Habinger, Wien 2015.

Butler 1920: H. C. Butler, Syria. Publications of the Princeton University Archaeological Expeditions to Syria in 1904-5. Division II: Architecture, Section B: Northern Syria, Leyden 1920.

Butler 1929: H. C. Butler, Early churches in Syria, Princeton 1929.

Lassus 1935-36: J. Lassus, Inventaire archéologique de la région au nord-est de Hama. Documents d´études orientales IV, vol. I-II Damaskus 1935-1936.

Loosely Lemming – Tchalenko 2019: E. Loosely Lemming – J. Tchalenko, Symeon Stylites at Qalʿat Simʿān, Text and Studies in Eastern Christianity, Vol. XII, Leiden 2019.

Mango 2010: M. M. Mango, Androna in Syria: Questions of environment and economy, in: F. Daim – J. Drauschke (Hrsg.), Byzanz. Das Römerreich im Mittelalter 2,1: Schauplätze. Monographien RGZM 84, 2, 1, Mainz 2010, 245-290.

Mouterde – Poidebard 1945: R. Mouterde – A. Poidebard, Le Limes de Chalkis. Organisation de la steppe en Haute-Syrie Romaine, Paris 1945.

Naccache 1992: A. Naccache, Le décor des églises de villages d´Antiochène du IVe au VIIe siècle, Paris 1992.

Schlimbach 2020: F. Schlimbach, Neue Forschungen in al-Andarīn. Das Ensemble der ‚Hauptkirche' von *Androna*, Heidelberg 2020.

Strube 1977: Ch. Strube, Die Formgebung der Apsisdekoration in Qalbloze und Qalat Siman, Jahrbuch für Antike und Christentum 20, 1977, 181-191.

Strube 1983: Ch. Strube, Die Kapitelle von Qasr ibn Wardan, Jahrbuch für Antike und Christentum 26, 1983, 59-106.

Strube 1993: Ch. Strube, Baudekoration im Nordsyrischen Kalksteinmassiv I. Kapitell-, Tür- und Gesimsformen des 4. und 5. Jahrhunderts n. Chr., Damaszener Forschungen 5, Mainz 1993.

Strube 2002: Ch. Strube, Baudekoration im Nordsyrischen Kalksteinmassiv II. Das 6. und frühe 7. Jahrhundert, Damaszener Forschungen 11, Mainz 2002.

Strube 2010: Ch. Strube, Al Andarin, das antike Androna, in: F. Daim – J. Drauschke (Hrsg.), Byzanz. Das Römerreich im Mittelalter 2, 1: Schauplätze. Monographien RGZM 84, 2, 1, Mainz 2010, 211-243.

Strube 2015, I-II: Ch. Strube, Al Andarin, das antike Androna. Oberflächenbefunde und Grabungsergebnisse: Die Umfassungsmauern und das Kastron, Monographie des RGZM 121, Mainz 2015.

Strube 2019: Ch. Strube, Das antike Androna. Zerstörungen durch den IS in Al Andarin, Antike Welt 3.19, 2019, 67-75.

Tchalenko 1953, I-III: G. Tchalenko, Villages antiques de la Syrie du Nord. Institut Français de Beyrouth, Bibliothèque archéologique et historique 50, vol. I-III Paris 1953.

Tchalenko 1980-1990: G. Tchalenko, Églises syriennes à bêma, I Texte (1990), II Planches (1979), III Album (1980).

de Vogüé 1865-1877, I-II: M. de Vogüé, Syrie centrale: Architecture civile et religieuse du Ier au VIIe siècle, vol. I-II Paris 1865–1877.

Tafeln / Plates 1-42

Die Abbildungen auf den Tafeln sind von der Autorin, mit folgenden Ausnahmen:
The illustrations on the plates are by the author, with the following exceptions:

Taf. / Pl. 2:	Tchalenko 1953 II, Pl. XXXIX
Taf. / Pl. 3:	Tchalenko 1953 II, Pl. CLIII
Taf. / Pl. 8b:	K. Leukefeld
Taf. / Pl. 9c:	K. Leukefeld
Taf. / Pl. 10b:	U. Hess
Taf. / Pl. 11b:	G. Tchalenko
Taf. / Pl. 12b:	Syrians for Heritage Association
Taf. / Pl. 13a. b:	Syrians for Heritage Association
Taf. / Pl. 15a:	Syrians for Heritage Association
Taf. / Pl. 15b:	T. Alhlo
Taf. / Pl. 17:	Strube 2015, I, 6 Abb. 3
Taf. / Pl. 18:	O. Hofmeister
Taf. / Pl. 19:	G. Gerster
Taf. / Pl. 21b:	U. Hess
Taf. / Pl. 26:	Strube 2015, II, Taf. 149
Taf. / Pl. 29:	K. Leukefeld
Taf. / Pl. 30b:	K. Leukefeld
Taf. / Pl. 31c:	K. Leukefeld
Taf. / Pl. 33a. b:	H. Hirth
Taf. / Pl. 34a. b. c:	H. Hirth
Taf. / Pl. 36a. b:	H. Hirth
Taf. / Pl. 37a:	n. n.
Taf. / Pl. 37c:	U. Hess
Taf. / Pl. 38a. b:	U. Hess
Taf. / Pl. 39b:	U. Hess
Taf. / Pl. 40a:	U. Hess

Tafel / Plate 1

Hama. Die Altstadt im Jahr 1980. a: Außenansicht, b: Innenansicht.

Hama. The old town in 1980. a: Outside view, b: Inside view.

Tafel / Plate 2

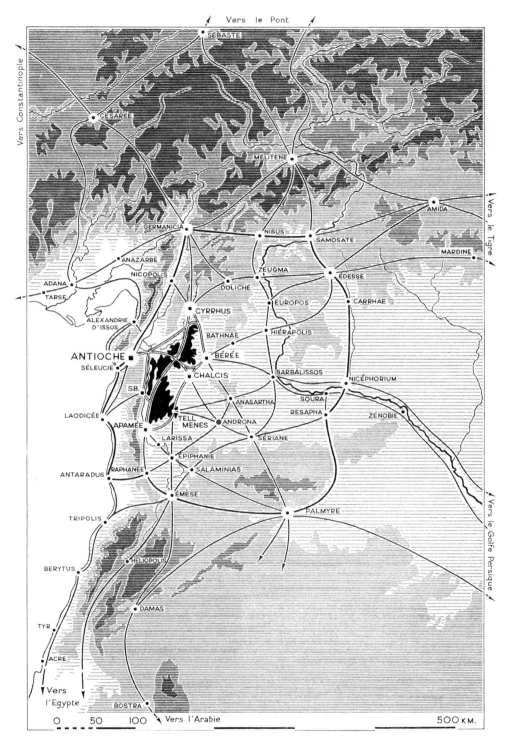

Syrienkarte von G. Tchalenko. Das Kalksteinmassiv ist schwarz eingetragen, al-Andarin ist mit rotem Punkt markiert.

Map of Syria by G. Tchalenko. The Limestone Massif in black, al-Andarin with a red point.

Tafel / Plate 3

Syrienkarte von G. Tchalenko. Die Karte mit den Klosteranlagen enthält alle im folgenden genannten Ruinenorte.

Map of Syria by G. Tchalenko. The map of the monasteries shows all ancient sites mentioned in the text.

Tafel / Plate 4

a

b

Beirut, Sammlung Henri Pharaon. a–b: Kapitelle aus Syrien in den Gartenanlagen.

Beirut, Henri Pharaon collection. a–b: Syrian capitals in the garden.

Tafel / Plate 5

Djebel Barisha. a: Die Siedlung Banaqfur im Frühling, b: Kalksteinfelsen bei Banaqfur.

Djebel Barisha: a: The ancient site Banaqfur in springtime, b: Limestonerock near Banaqfur.

Tafel / Plate 6

Qalʿat Simʿan. a: Nordansicht des kreuzförmigen Baukomplexes, b: Der ursprüngliche Weg hinauf zu den Bauten des Pilgerzentrums.

Qalʿat Simʿan. a: The building complex from the North, b: The original way up to the pilgrimage centre.

Tafel / Plate 7

a: El Bara. Ansicht des Ruinenortes mit Weinanbau im Vordergrund, b: Deir Sambul. Innenansicht der Kirche; Fundlage der Kapitelle.

a: El Bara. View of the ancient site with viticulture in the foreground, b: Deir Sambul. Interior of the church with capitals.

Tafel / Plate 8

Aleppo, Madrasa al-Hallawiya. a: Erhaltungszustand im Jahr 1979, b: Zerstörter Westteil im Jahr 2014.

Aleppo, Madrasa al-Hallawiya. a: The situation of the church in 1979, b: The western part after its destruction in 2014.

Aleppo, Madrasa al-Hallawiya. a–b: Detaillierte Aufnahmen der Kapitelle der westlichen Säulenstellung, c: Innenansicht nach den Zerstörungen 2014.

Aleppo, Madrasa al-Hallawiyya. a–b: Detailed documentation of the capitals on the western side, c: Interior view after the destructions in 2014.

Tafel / Plate 10

Qasr ibn Wardan. a: Kirche und Residenz während der Restaurierung 1979, b: Scheich Abu Hussein mit seinem Vater und Enkelkindern.

Qasr ibn Wardan. a: Church and residence in restoration in 1979, b: Sheik Abu Hussein with his father and grandchildren.

Tafel / Plate 11

Qalʿat Simʿan. a: Ansicht des Pilgerzentrums von Norden, b: Die von G. Tchalenko restaurierte Südfassade, Zustand 1938.

Qalʿat Simʿan. a: View of the pilgrimage-centre from the North, b: The southern façade restored by G. Tchalenko, in 1938.

Tafel / Plate 12

Qal'at Sim'an. a: Die Südfassade im Jahr 1975, b: Die Südfassade nach den Zerstörungen 2014–2016.

Qal'at Sim'an. a: The southern façade in 1975, b: The southern facade after the destructions 2014–2016.

Tafel / Plate 13

Qalʿat Simʿan. a: Südfassade mit Zerstörung der östlichen Säule des zentralen Eingangsbogens im Jahr 2016, b: Südlicher Kreuzarm von Südosten im Jahr 2016.

Qalʿat Simʿan. a: Southern facade with the column of the great arch damaged, b: Southern part of the cruciform building from Southeast in 2016.

Tafel / Plate 14

Qalʿat Simʿan. a: Ostfassade des südlichen Kreuzarms im Jahr 1975, b: Das Oktogon. Blick von der Simeonssäule aus in die Ostkirche und den Nordarm. Zustand im Jahr 1975.

Qalʿat Simʿan. a: The eastern facade of the southern basilica, b: The octogonal centre with the stylites column. View into the eastern and northern basilicas. Situation in 1975.

Tafel / Plate 15

Qalʿat Simʿan. a: Das Podium der Simeonssäule mit Blick in die Ostkirche und den Südarm, Zustand 2016, b: Blick vom zerstörten Podium aus zur Westbasilika, Zustand 2016.

Qalʿat Simʿan. a: The base of the stylite's column and view into the eastern and southern basilicas in 2016, b: View from the destroyed base of the stylite's column into the western basilica in 2016.

Tafel / Plate 16

a–b.: Qal'at Sim'an. a: Apsisdekoration der Ostbasilika, b: Kapitell der Ostkirche, c: Deir Sambul, Kapitell der Kirche (vgl. Taf. 7b).

a–b: Qal'at Sim'an. a: The eastern basilica, decoration of the apse, b: Capital of the eastern basilica, c: Deir Sambul, capital of the church (cf. Pl. 7b).

Tafel / Plate 17

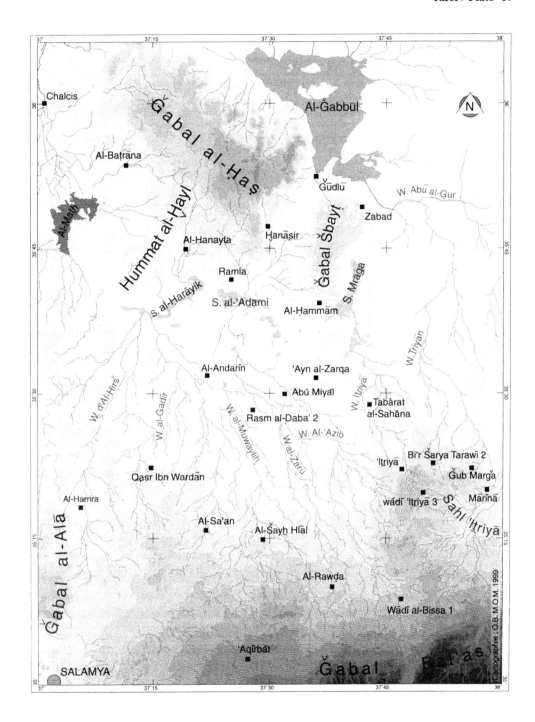

Karte Syriens mit der großen inneren Ebene und den Orten al-Andarin, Qasr ibn Wardan und al-Hamra.

Map of Syria with the great central plain, showing the sites al-Andarin, Qasr ibn Wardan and al-Hamra.

Tafel / Plate 18

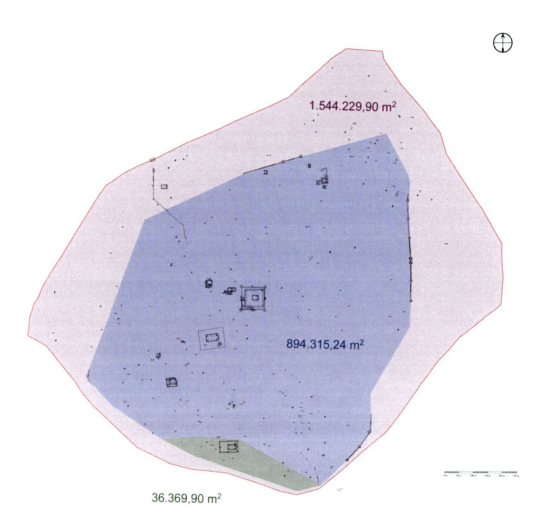

Al-Andarin / Androna. Die erste Phase der Siedlung, eingefasst von einer Basaltmauer, und die Erweiterung, eingefasst von einer Umfassungsmauer aus Lehmziegeln (O. Hofmeister).

Al-Andarin / Androna. The original site with a circuitwall in basalt, and the enlarged site with a circuitwall in sunbaken bricks (O. Hofmeister).

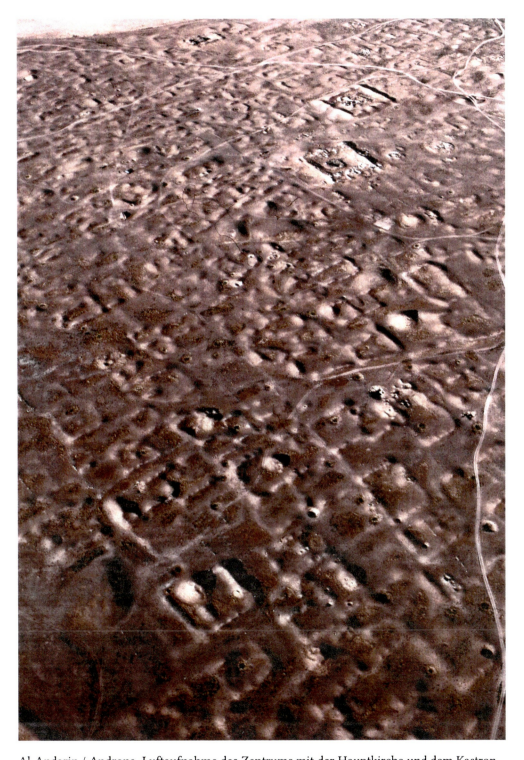

Al-Andarin / Androna. Luftaufnahme des Zentrums mit der Hauptkirche und dem Kastron.

Al-Andarin / Androna. Aerial photograph of the central region with the main church and the kastron.

Tafel / Plate 20

Al-Andarin / Androna. a: Bohrung nach Grundwasser, b: Der Grabungsarchitekt O. Hofmeister, c: Bau des Grabungshauses.

Al-Andarin / Androna. a: The first jet of groundwater, b: The architect O. Hofmeister, c: Construction of the excavation house.

Tafel / Plate 21

Al-Andarin / Androna. a: Fertigstellung des Grabungshauses, b: Die Terrasse des Grabungshauses mit Feldbetten.

Al-Andarin / Androna. a: The excavation house is finished, b: The terrace of the excavation house with camp-beds.

Tafel / Plate 22

Al-Andarin / Androna. a: Kastron. Anfang der Grabungsarbeiten auf den Erd- und Sandschichten des Westteils (vgl. Taf. 30a), b: Kastron. Endstadium der Grabungsarbeiten: das Westtor, das Rampenhaus, die Südhalle und der südwestliche Eckturm.

Al-Andarin / Androna. a: Kastron. The first days of excavation on the western side (cf. Pl. 30a), b: The Kastron, final stage of the excavations: the western door, the ramphouse, the southern hall and the southwestern tower.

Al-Andarin / Androna. a: Die frühbyzantinische Badanlage, b: Die omayyadische Badanlage.

Al-Andarin / Androna. a: The byzantine bath, b: The omayyad bath.

Tafel / Plate 24

a

b

Al-Andarin / Androna. a: Der Hauskomplex von Südosten, b: Eingangstür auf der Südseite des Hauses.

Al-Andarin / Androna. a: The byzantine house, view from the Southeast, b: Entrance door on the southern side of the byzantine house.

Tafel / Plate 25

Al-Andarin / Androna. a: Eingangsbereich des Hauskomplexes, b: Ausschnitt aus dem Bodenmosaik im Empfangsraum.

Al-Andarin / Androna. a: Vestibule ot the byzantine house, b: Scene in the mosaic floor of the reception hall.

Tafel / Plate 26

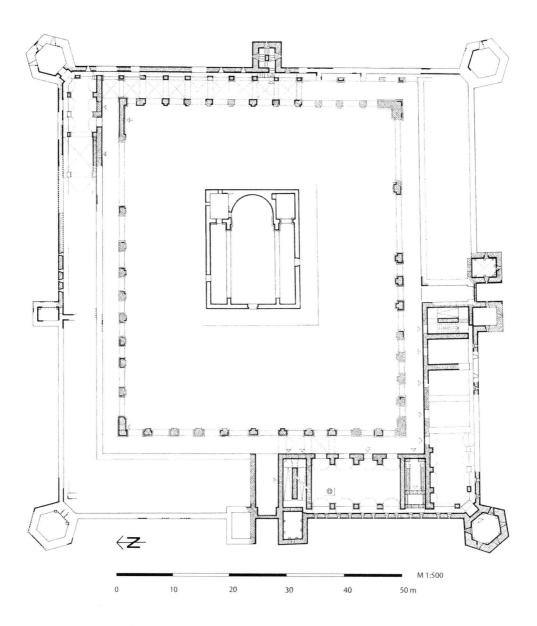

Al-Andarin / Androna. Grundriss des Kastrons.

Al-Andarin / Androna. Groundplan of the kastron.

Al-Andarin / Androna. a–b: Kastron. Restaurierung des Westtores und des Turmes an seiner Südseite.

Al-Andarin / Androna. a–b: Kastron. Restoration of the western door and the flanking tower on its southern side.

Tafel / Plate 28

a

b

Al-Andarin / Androna. a–b: Kastron. Das Westtor und die Westhalle nach der Restaurierung.

Al-Andarin / Androna. a–b: Kastron. The western gate and the western hall after restoration.

Tafel / Plate 29

Al-Andarin / Androna, Kastron. Das Westtor nach der Zerstörung im Jahr 2016.

Al-Andarin / Androna, Kastron. The western gate after its destruction in 2016.

Al-Andarin / Androna, Kastron. a: Die Westhalle im Jahr 2003, im Hintergrund die beiden Badanlagen, b: Die Westhalle im Jahr 2016.

Al-Andarin / Androna, Kastron. a: The western hall in 2003, with the byzantine and the omayyad baths in the background, b: The western hall in 2016.

Tafel / Plate 31

Al-Andarin / Androna, Kastron. a–b: Ansichten der Südhalle vor der Zerstörung 2016, c: Trümmerberg mit Fragment einer Basalttür im Jahr 2016.

Al-Andarin / Androna, Kastron. a–b: Views of the southern hall before its destruction in 2016, c: Heap of ruins with fragment of a basalt door in 2016.

Tafel / Plate 32

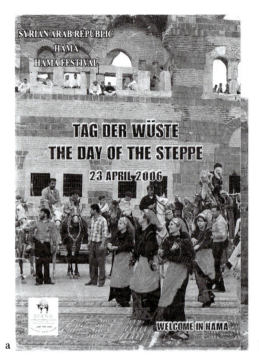
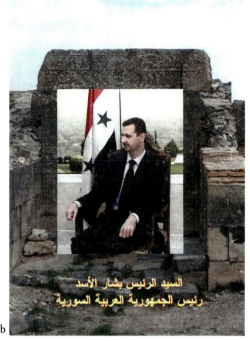

Al-Andarin / Androna. a: Broschüre zum ‚Tag der Wüste / Steppe', Titelblatt, b: ebd., Baschar al Assad im Westtor des Kastrons sitzend, c: Die Kirche im Hof des Kastrons.

Al-Andarin / Androna. a: Booklet for the ‚Day of the desert / steppe', frontispiece, b: *ibid.*, Baschar al Assad sitting in the opening of the western gate of the kastron, c: The church in the court of the kastron.

Tafel / Plate 33

Al-Andarin / Androna. a: Ein blauer VW-Käfer im Zentrum Andronas, b: Der Bogen der Hauptkirche zusammen mit dem blauen Käfer auf den Ostereiern im Jahr 2007.

Al-Andarin / Androna. a: A blue VW Beetle in the centre of Androna, b: The main church of Androna together with the blue car on the easter eggs in 2007.

Tafel / Plate 34

a: Aleppo. Mudira beim Kauf von Trüffeln, b: Al-Andarin / Androna. Champignons im Lehmziegelhügel der Hausgrabung, c: Sroudj. Festessen im Haus von Chalid al Taki mit der Kommissarin Wafa Zaqqour, Ph. Niewöhner, U. Hess und I. Eichner.

a: Aleppo. Mudira buying truffles, b: Al-Andarin / Androna. Champignons in the loamhills of the byzantine house, c: Sroudj. Feast in the house of Chalid al Taki together with the commissioner Wafa Zaqqour, Ph. Niewöhner, U. Hess and I. Eichner.

a: Stabl Antar. C. Mango unterwegs, b: Al-Andarin / Androna. C. Mango und R. Hoyland, c: Hama. Marlia und Cyril Mango gemeinsam mit dem deutschen Team im Restaurant an den Wasserrädern.

a: Stabl Antar. C. Mango on his walk, b: Al-Andarin / Androna. C. Mango and R. Hoyland, c: Hama. Marlia and Cyril Mango. A feast in the restaurant at the nourias together with the German team.

Tafel / Plate 36

Al-Andarin / Androna. a–b: O. Hofmeister und E. Winckelmann, Mitarbeiter des deutschen Teams im Haus von Adnan Sammakiya und vor dem Wasserbassin der neu angelegten Felder.

Al-Andarin / Androna. a–b: O. Hofmeister and E. Winckelmann, members ot the German team in the house of Adnan Sammakiya and visiting the waterbasin of the cultivated fields.

a–b: Bashmishli. a: G. Tchalenko im Jahr 1940, b: Der Antikenwächter Abu Feisal (rechts) und Abu Abdu (links) im Jahr 1989, c: El Bara. C. S. mit Th. Rhode, Abu Aboud und seinem Onkel.

a–b: Bashmishli. a: G. Tchalenko in 1940, b: The antiquities guardian Abu Feisal (right) together with Abu Abdu (left) in 1989, c: El Bara. C. S. together with Th. Rhode, Abou Aboud and his uncle.

Al-Andarin / Androna. a: Mudira mit Abu Achmed und Nassar aus Djenad, b: Gruppenfoto mit Waʻal Haffian, H. Hirth, I. Eichner, P. Knötzele, M. Seibel und A. Ade.

Al-Andarin / Androna. a: Mudira together with Abu Achmed and Nassar from Djenad, b: Group photograph of Waʻal Haffian, H. Hirth, I. Eichner, P. Knötzele, M. Seibel and A. Ade.

a

b

Al-Andarin / Androna. a: Die Köchin Umm Saleh, b: Gruppenfoto mit den Restauratoren sowie S. Mehret, I. Eichner, E. Winckelmann und K. Malige.

Al-Andarin / Androna. a: The cook Umm Saleh, b: Group photograph of the restorers, together with S. Mehret, I. Eichner, E. Winckelmann and K. Malige.

Tafel / Plate 40

Al-Andarin / Androna. a: Gruppenfoto mit G. Ateş, Chalid al Taki und lokalen Mitarbeitern der Grabung, b: Ch. Ewert zusammen mit Mitgliedern des deutschen Teams.

Al-Andarin / Androna. a: Group photograph of G. Ateş, Chalid al Taki and local workers of the excavation, b: Ch. Ewert together with members of the German team.

Al-Andarin / Androna. a: Die Grabungsarchitektin U. Hess mit Hussein aus Qasr ibn Wardan, b: Die beiden Architekten O. Hofmeister und A. Leibhammer.

Al-Andarin / Androna. a: U. Hess, the architect of the excavation team together with Hussein of Qasr ibn Wardan, b: The architects O. Hofmeister and A. Leibhammer.

Tafel / Plate 42

Al-Andarin / Androna. a: R. Bielfeldt, F. Schlimbach und A. Arbeiter im Steingarten der Hausgrabung, b: F. Schlimbach auf dem Mosaik des byzantinischen Hauses.

Al-Andarin / Androna. a: R. Bielfeldt, F. Schlimbach and A. Arbeiter in the stonegarden of the byzantine house, b: F. Schlimbach on the mosaic of the byzantine house.

Druck und Bindung
Books on Demand GmbH
In de Tarpen 42, 22848 Norderstedt